Humanitarianism Contested

This book provides a succinct but sophisticated understanding of humanitarianism, and insight into the ongoing dilemmas and tensions that have accompanied it since its origins in the early nineteenth century. Combining theoretical and historical exposition with a broad range of contemporary case studies, the book:

- surveys the evolution of humanitarianism, beginning with the early nineteenth century and continuing to today's challenge of post-conflict reconstruction and saving failed states;
- explains how humanitarianism has exploded in scope, scale, and significance;
- presents an overview of the contemporary humanitarian sector, including briefly who the key actors are, how they are funded, and what they do with their money;
- analyzes the ethical dilemmas confronted by humanitarian organizations, not only in the abstract but also, and most importantly, in real situations and when lives are at stake; and
- examines how humanitarianism poses fundamental ethical questions regarding the kind of world we want to live in, what kind of world is possible, and how we might get there.

An accessible and engaging work by two of the leading scholars in the field, *Humanitarianism Contested* is essential reading for all those concerned with the future of human rights and international relations.

Michael Barnett is University Professor of International Affairs and Political Science at the George Washington University.

Thomas G. Weiss is Presidential Professor of Political Science at The Graduate Center of The City University of New York and Director of the Ralph Bunche Institute for International Studies.

Routledge Global Institutions

Edited by Thomas G. Weiss
The CUNY Graduate Center, New York, USA
and Rorden Wilkinson
University of Manchester, UK

About the series

The "Global Institutions" series is designed to provide readers with comprehensive, accessible, and informative guides to the history, structure, and activities of key international organizations as well as books that deal with topics of key importance in contemporary global governance. Every volume stands on its own as a thorough and insightful treatment of a particular topic, but the series as a whole contributes to a coherent and complementary portrait of the phenomenon of global institutions at the dawn of the millennium.

Books are written by recognized experts, conform to a similar structure, and cover a range of themes and debates common to the series. These areas of shared concern include the general purpose and rationale for organizations, developments over time, membership, structure, decision-making procedures, and key functions. Moreover, current debates are placed in historical perspective alongside informed analysis and critique. Each book also contains an annotated bibliography and guide to electronic information as well as any annexes appropriate to the subject matter at hand.

The volumes currently published are:

51 Humanitarianism Contested (2011)
Where angels fear to tread
by Michael Barnett (George Washington University) and Thomas G. Weiss (The CUNY Graduate Center)

50 The Organization of American States (2011)
Global governance away from the media
by Monica Herz (Institute of International Relations, Catholic University, Rio de Janeiro)

49 Non-Governmental Organizations in World Politics (2011)
The construction of global governance
by Peter Willetts (City University, London)

Books currently under contract include:

The Regional Development Banks
Lending with a regional flavor
by Jonathan R. Strand (University of Nevada)

Millennium Development Goals (MDGs)
For a people-centered development agenda?
by Sakiko Fukada-Parr (The New School)

Peacebuilding
From concept to commission
by Robert Jenkins (The CUNY Graduate Center)

Human Security
by Don Hubert (University of Ottawa)

UNICEF
by Richard Jolly (University of Sussex)

FIFA
by Alan Tomlinson (University of Brighton)

International Law, International Relations, and Global Governance
by Charlotte Ku (University of Illinois)

The Bank for International Settlements
The politics of global financial supervision in the age of high finance
by Kevin Ozgercin (SUNY College at Old Westbury)

International Migration
by Khalid Koser (Geneva Centre for Security Policy)

Global Health Governance
by Sophie Harman (City University, London)

The Council of Europe
by Martyn Bond (University of London)

Human Development
by Richard Ponzio

The United Nations Development Programme and System (UNDP)
by Stephen Browne (The International Trade Centre, Geneva)

For further information regarding the series, please contact:

Craig Fowlie, Senior Publisher, Politics & International Studies
Taylor & Francis
2 Park Square, Milton Park, Abingdon
Oxon OX14 4RN, UK

+44 (0)207 842 2057 Tel
+44 (0)207 842 2302 Fax

Craig.Fowlie@tandf.co.uk
www.routledge.com

Humanitarianism Contested

Where angels fear to tread

Michael Barnett and Thomas G. Weiss

Routledge
Taylor & Francis Group

LONDON AND NEW YORK

First published 2011
by Routledge
2 Park Square, Milton Park, Abingdon, Oxon, OX14 4RN

Simultaneously published in the U.S.A. and Canada
by Routledge
711 Third Avenue, New York, NY 10017

Routledge is an imprint of the Taylor & Francis Group, an informa business

British Library Cataloguing in Publication Data
A catalogue record for this book is available from the British Library

Library of Congress Cataloging in Publication Data
Barnett, Michael N., 1960–
    Humanitarianism contested : where angels fear to tread / Michael Barnett
and Thomas G. Weiss.
        p. cm. – (Routledge global institutions ; 51)
    Includes bibliographical references and index.
    1. Humanitarian assistance. 2. Humanitarianism. 3. International relief. I.
Weiss, Thomas George II. Title.
    HV553.B36 2011
    361.7–dc22
    2010037784

ISBN: 978-0-415-49663-6 (hbk)
ISBN: 978-0-415-49664-3 (pbk)
ISBN: 978-0-203-82930-1 (ebk)

Typeset in Times New Roman by
Taylor & Francis Books

Contents

Foreword

Humanitarianism in the crossfire

Jan Egeland

Early one Saturday morning in August 2010, the bullet-riddled bodies of 10 relief workers—three of them women—were found along a road in the Badakshan province of eastern Afghanistan. "Before their travel we warned them not to tour near jungles in Nuristan, but they said they were doctors and no one was going to hurt them," the local Afghan police chief told Reuters.[1]

The execution of unarmed, civilian humanitarian workers is a stark reminder of how humanitarian action struggles to survive in the political and literal cross-fires of our time and age. It also graphically shows the nature and challenges of current relief work—how globalized, politicized, exposed, and vulnerable relief operations have become.

In the context of a decade-old, poorly executed Western military campaign in a feudal Islamic society, a Western faith-based group, International Assistance Mission, has its staff murdered under the stated pretext that the victims "had been trying to convert Muslims." The ruthless Taliban made this claim and have publicly declared that they respect none of the international legal or humanitarian principles established during many generations of international humanitarian operations. The losers in this latest of many tragedies for humanitarian work are not only the butchered American, British, German, and Afghan doctors and relief workers, but also Afghanistan's civilian population who are increasingly out of reach for humanitarianism.

Access denied

International terrorism and the so-called war on terror can explain some of this crisis for the right of unimpeded humanitarian access to victims of armed conflicts and disasters. The ability to obtain and maintain access to populations in need is a prerequisite for national and international humanitarian agencies. Without it, they cannot deliver humanitarian assistance or protect vulnerable populations. While most countries remain safe for relief work, an increasing number of war zones are becoming ever more dangerous.

The vast majority of physical attacks on aid workers in the past decade have occurred in Afghanistan, Chad, Iraq, Pakistan, Somalia, Sri Lanka, and Sudan. In particular, it is national staff of UN agencies and non-governmental organizations (NGOs) who bear the brunt of this risk. Moreover, perceptions of affiliations with political and military agendas have eroded acceptance of humanitarian actors. The core humanitarian principles of impartiality, neutrality, humanity, and independence are not honored. The protective nature of the emblems of the United Nations, the Red Cross and Red Crescent societies, and humanitarian organizations have been undermined.[2] Perhaps the most obvious indication was the September 2003 delivery of a bomb to the International Committee of the Red Cross's headquarters in Baghdad via a white ambulance with a red crescent symbol.

Man walked on the moon more than a generation ago, but we are still far away from securing even an absolute minimum of predictable international relief and protection for civilians in many of the wars and crises of our time. Too many communities are neither a strategic concern nor a public opinion priority in the world's leading capitals or among the political, economic, and military elites who could make a difference.

I have been a humanitarian worker, researcher, and activist for more than 30 years. More often than not, I have felt that whether or not our appeals for desperate people were heard reflects the results of a bizarre lottery for international attention rather than a rights-based response of objective needs and global resources.

If you are African, non-English speaking, and affected by a slow-onset natural disaster or a protracted ongoing conflict, you will lose in the Western media, and in Washington, London, and Scandinavian capitals that are best able to place humanitarian priorities on the international agenda. The net short-term outcome of deliberations among these countries is too often funding for a minimum of blankets and band-aids to keep people alive but not for the comprehensive investment in development, security, justice, and politics that underpin solutions that could help people escape vicious circles of misery and vulnerability.

Think before you act

In *Humanitarianism Contested: Where angels fear to tread*, two of the world's leading analysts of international relations and organizations, Michael Barnett and Thomas G. Weiss, team up to draw a roadmap for the embattled yet increasingly important life-saving humanitarian sector.

Nearly 150 years after Henry Dunant founded the International Committee of the Red Cross and humanitarian law, idealistic do-gooders are hunted down by political extremists and their work is politicized and misused by friendly as well as unfriendly governments and donors. That is why we need global experts like Barnett and Weiss to explain how historical, political, organizational, and cultural forces come together in today's lethal cocktail for relief workers and their beneficiaries.

Barnett and Weiss spell out clearly why humanitarian action too often does not seem to be on the side of angels. They explain how and why many efforts to make a real difference for the neediest are frustrated. Only fools would rush in without thinking and reflecting about the context and consequences of action and non-action. Here is a short, sharp, and indispensable volume that will help students and practitioners alike to think and analyze as well as, when needed, rush to the rescue. The two authors believe there is a way, long and winding, that leads out of the current quagmire, and they tell us how to get from here to there. Indeed, this book is required reading for those interested in understanding the profound changes in world politics and humanitarian action during the last two decades.

Progress on our watch

During my years as global emergency relief coordinator and UN under-secretary-general for humanitarian affairs, I witnessed the strengths and weakness of international compassion on our watch. I saw UN and nongovernmental humanitarian efforts in most of our generation's wars and large-scale disasters. It was my job to mobilize attention, gather resources, and try to promote positive change in the face of disasters and armed conflicts. Coordinating humanitarian action within the world organization, and between the UN and other governmental and nongovernmental humanitarian agencies, meant that I had access to all the actors, good and bad, but could not order anyone to do anything unless they were convinced it was right.[3]

From 2003 to 2006, I witnessed first-hand how effective multilateral action with local and regional partners helped build progress and peace. Wars ended and hope was provided in Liberia and Sierra Leone, Angola and Burundi, southern Sudan and northern Uganda, Kosovo and Nepal. Through the United Nations, we also coordinated massive, life-saving international relief in the Indian Ocean tsunami, the South Asian earthquake, the Horn of Africa, Southern Africa, the Lebanon war, and the Darfur crisis. In several of these overwhelming emergencies, hundreds of thousands of lives were predicted to perish. The sombre predictions were averted because humanitarian action, building on local capacities, was infinitely more effective than a generation ago.

So in spite of the overwhelming challenges that Barnett and Weiss describe so powerfully in this volume, I believe that we have made and can make further progress on our watch. The world is, in spite of setbacks and international economic recession and political crisis, getting steadily better for the majority of us. There is more peace, and more children get education and health care than when the Cold War ended. Fewer children die, even with a growing world population. Due to more effective disaster risk reduction and more and better humanitarian organizations, fewer people perish in the growing number of natural disasters.[4] The number of armed conflicts has gone from more than 50 to less than 40 since the early 1990s. There is a marked increase in life expectancy on all continents and in most nations. There are many more democracies, fewer military coups, and less genocide than a generation ago.[5]

Injustice in our time

While the glass is over half full, there is also a darker side to globalization: the world is more socially unjust than in previous generations as the distance between the top and the bottom billion has increased dramatically. The affluent nations and the richest within nations have become rich beyond the wildest imaginations of our forefathers. But the poorest two billion live in the same abject misery as before and on less than two dollars a day.[6]

While fewer civilians are killed in wars now than 10 or 20 years ago, the brutality of armed actors and the suffering of the defenseless remain medieval. The pattern of violence and the atrocities that I saw in Afghanistan, Iraq, and Gaza are too similar to what I have seen in the Congo, Ivory Coast, Kosovo, Darfur, Chad, Colombia, Chechnya, and other places where fighting takes place amidst and often against the civilian population. I saw, time and again, how in our time, it is more dangerous to be a woman or a child in these battlefields than an armed adult male soldier.

Westernized humanitarianism

There is a near-consensus across the political, cultural, and religious spectra that we need to protect and promote effective assistance to the most vulnerable populations in times of crisis and conflict. We know for a fact that all world religions promote ideals of compassion, justice, and respect for the dignity of life. No religion condones or approves the killing of innocents. But all major religions have been exploited to justify violence and intolerance by extremists—and in this generation, especially on the fringes of some Islamic groups and sects.

The danger is that humanitarianism, a universal imperative and shared intercultural system of principles, has become so Westernized in its funding, staffing, organizational structure, and political profile that it risks long-term adversity in many non-Western settings. In addition, we often see the wrong countries push the right causes and thus undermine the effectiveness of action. When Burma's military rulers block life-saving aid to their own people, it should immediately fall upon China, India, and their neighbors in ASEAN (Association of Southeast Asian Nations) to take the lead in convincing the regime to provide for international access. The ball falls in their court because these Asian economic powers have real leverage, as opposed to the West with visible resources and condemnation.

I noticed similarly when we tried in 2003–6 to mobilize against the atrocities in Darfur that there was little help or interest among Sudan's Asian or Arab trading partners. That neglect became fateful because they might have made an impact in Khartoum—as opposed to Westerners who failed. Once, when I protested to government officials the massive rape of women in Darfur, they counterattacked: "We see your criticism in Western media, but we also see who support you: the same nations that tear apart Iraq and betray the Palestinians—and you want us to take moral lessons from them?" The road of international solidarity and diplomacy has been paved by examples of wrong countries pushing right causes, while the potentially influential ones become passive bystanders.

Humanitarian reform

In 2005, as the global emergency relief coordinator, I initiated an ambitious reform effort. This effort of change management was triggered by the initially weak UN and NGO response to the humanitarian needs in Darfur in 2004. In the UN Office for the Coordination of Humanitarian Affairs, we had ample proof that our old systems for funding, preparedness, and coordination did not perform as they should. We were simply too slow to come to the rescue of the 1 million displaced in western Sudan, even after June 2004 when our pressure succeeded in lifting many of the Sudanese government's restrictions on our access. Even with the so-called CNN-effect working on our side and ministers coming to our fundraising meetings, during several long months we got too few experienced logisticians, water engineers, camp managers, and protection experts on the ground inside Darfur.

Knowing that it is usually easier to get forgiveness than permission, I decided to start up the reform process with humanitarian colleagues immediately and ask for formal approvals later. A humanitarian response review was undertaken by experienced experts interviewing operational organizations and field workers. UN agencies and NGOs agreed that the reform should boost our humanitarian muscles by ensuring pre-dictability, accountability, and partnership. In effect, we reached more beneficiaries with more comprehensive needs-based relief and protection, in a more effective and timely manner.

The humanitarian reform program was launched at the end of 2005 with several key pillars. First, we agreed through the humanitarian Inter-Agency Standing Committee (IASC, composed of UN agencies, three large NGO federations, and the Red Cross and Red Crescent Movement) to establish a series of operational partnerships that we coined the "cluster" approach. These clusters have since been set up in most large emergencies to improve coordination in such areas as water and sanitation, emergency health, logistics, shelter, and protection of the civilian population. We asked individual operational agencies to take the lead in each of these clusters and ensure that materials and expertise were planned, mobilized, and applied to good effect.

When we started reform efforts, our response capacity varied hugely from one area and population to another. More often than not food was effectively provided through the World Food Programme, but tons of corn or lentils are of no use to a mother if her child is dying from the lack of clean water. It was therefore important that UNICEF, partnering with NGOs, took responsibility for providing water supplies and latrines in a more predictable manner, as other agencies con-centrated on other gap areas. The cluster approach is slowly, but surely, having the effect of providing more predictable assistance for more people in more places.

Second, we needed more predictable funding, not so much for media-exposed "loud" emergencies such as the Indian Ocean tsunami, Darfur, and the Lebanon war in 2006, but rather for forgotten or "silent" emergencies without public opinion attention. Secretary-General Kofi Annan proposed that the 2005 UN World Summit set up a new and expanded Central Emergency Response Fund (CERF) aiming at $500 million in voluntary contributions from member states. We secured important support from the governments of the United Kingdom,

Sweden, Norway, and Luxemburg, who were willing to invest in and campaign for a fund that could guarantee that we had "water in our hose when a fire was detected," to quote British development minister Hilary Benn.[7]

When the proposal to establish the CERF came before the General Assembly in late 2005, it was already an uncontroversial fait accompli and the first element of the whole UN reform package to be agreed.[8] All regional groups had been consulted, donors had promised sufficient money to get going, and humanitarian organizations had been included in the planning process. Only four months later, the CERF was launched with an impressive initial $260 million from 48 governments and the private sector. Since then, more than $400 million annually has been raised and disbursed to neglected emergencies around the world.

Third, neither operational clusters nor efficient use of funding will occur without a guarantee of effective leadership on the ground. An additional pillar of the humanitarian reform therefore was a systematic effort to recruit and train a stand-by pool of highly qualified humanitarian coordinators for emergency relief operations. The work of these key "field marshals" has varied in terms of leadership and creativeness. Too often UN resident coordinators continued business-as-usual when they were also given emergency responsibilities. The number of trained and experienced candidates from inside and outside the UN system has been steadily expanded in recent years and can now be deployed to major disaster or conflict zones.

Finally, we started a process of broadening partnerships by trying to be less "UN-centric" and less "Northern." The United Nations system is engaged in larger and more numerous relief and recovery operations than ever before, but its relative share of the total humanitarian response is shrinking. The UN's comparative advantage is standard-setting, coordination, facilitation, and seeing that political, security, and humanitarian efforts come together. Most of the actual delivery of assistance on the ground is, however, undertaken by the growing number of NGOs and civil society movements from the North and increasingly from the South as well.

During the generous and global response to the Indian Ocean tsunami in 2004–5, more than 90 governments and millions of individuals and companies worldwide donated some $13 billion to relief and reconstruction. Thirty-five countries provided vital military and civil defense assets to immediate emergency operations. Some 300 international relief groups converged on Ache in Indonesia and Sri Lanka in the first month of the relief effort. This was clearly too many, perhaps even twice as many as what would have been most efficient. The local communities had their own organizations, and authorities were too often shunted aside and not consulted.

In the future we must think more strategically, and more locally, in the way that we undertake our long-term efforts to make societies resilient to hazards and strife. We must work more closely with local governments and civil society to strengthen their capacities for handling crises and governing. We must find better ways to forge partnership—internationally, nationally, and locally in order to tap effectively local resources and expertise.

Time and again we see that more lives are saved in earthquakes, floods, and tsunamis by local groups than by expensive airborne fire brigades. Similarly, it is usually local and regional actors who make or break peace-building and reconciliation. Recognizing the need to discuss a new deal in forging effective partnerships beyond borders and artificial organizational barriers, we convened a first meeting of executive leaders of leading humanitarian organizations from the North and the South and from UN and non-UN agencies to form a Global Humanitarian Platform in Geneva in 2006.[9] This work is continuing and expanding.

The growth in high-quality civil society movements, especially within Third World societies, is probably the single most important trend in global efforts to combat poverty and conflict. They are far more important than governments and intergovernmental organizations usually acknowledge.

Over the years, and in spite of often half-hearted investment by the powerful and the rich, we have succeeded in providing life-saving assistance and protection to those in greatest need. Through the United Nations and other international organizations, I have seen how we can organize, against all odds, tremendous processes of change when we have a sufficient minimum of political support from the most powerful capitals and a sufficient minimum of resources from the richest nations. So there is, in spite of all the troubles and threats, hope for humanitarian action. *Humanitarianism Contested* explains how and why. Always insightful and never losing perspective or a sense of the possible, Barnett and Weiss overcome the despair and naïvety of too much of the thinking and writing about contemporary humanitarian action.

Foreword by the series editor

The current volume is the fifty-first title in a dynamic series on global institutions. The series strives (and, based on the volumes published to date, succeeds) to provide readers with definitive guides to the most visible aspects of what many of us know as "global governance." Remarkable as it may seem, there exist relatively few books that offer in-depth treatments of prominent global bodies, processes, and associated issues, much less an entire series of concise and complementary volumes. Those that do exist are either out of date, inaccessible to the non-specialist reader, or seek to develop a specialized understanding of particular aspects of an institution or process rather than offer an overall account of its functioning. Similarly, existing books have often been written in highly technical language or have been crafted "in-house" and are notoriously self-serving and narrow.

The advent of electronic media has undoubtedly helped research and teaching by making data and primary documents of international organizations more widely available, but it has also complicated matters. The growing reliance on the Internet and other electronic methods of finding information about key international organizations and processes has served, ironically, to limit the educational and analytical materials to which most readers have ready access—namely, books. Public relations documents, raw data, and loosely refereed web sites do not make for intelligent analysis. Official publications compete with a vast amount of electronically available information, much of which is suspect because of its ideological or self-promoting slant. Paradoxically, a growing range of purportedly independent web sites offering analyses of the activities of particular organizations has emerged, but one inadvertent consequence has been to frustrate access to basic, authoritative, readable, critical, and well-researched texts. The market for such has actually been reduced by the ready availability of varying quality electronic materials.

For those of us who teach, research, and practice in the area, such limited access to information has been frustrating. We were delighted when Routledge saw the value of a series that bucks this trend and provides key reference points to the most significant global institutions and issues. They are betting that serious students and professionals will want serious analyses. We have assembled a first-rate line-up of authors to address that market. Our intention, then, is to provide one-stop shopping for all readers—students (both undergraduate and post-graduate), negotiators, diplomats, practitioners from nongovernmental and intergovernmental organizations, and interested parties alike—seeking information about the most prominent institutional aspects of global governance.

Humanitarianism contested

Humanitarianism is in something of a bind. Not only do too many widespread human rights violations, genocidal campaigns, mass killings, rapes, and tortures continue to pass by without effective international action (and in some cases, without any form of condemnation), the way in which we talk about humanitarianism is almost entirely unable to move beyond the stale and polarized debate about whether we should save strangers or not.[1] Indeed, the lack of concerted action in the face of a humanitarian emergency both enforces and is reinforced by the near universal inability of commentators, practitioners, and academics alike to move beyond entrenched positions about the principles guiding (non)intervention. The subtitle says it all: *Where angels fear to tread*—but Barnett and Weiss sprint ahead nonetheless.

If ever a field needed, as George Orwell put it of the English language, to "[cut] out all stale and mixed images, all prefabricated phrases, and humbug and vagueness"[2] and to replace it with data-based argumentation and serious political will, it is the field of humanitarianism. Had this been the case, the lives of hundreds of thousands would not have been lost in Rwanda while discursive sleights of hand were used to justify a lack of intervention and forestall recourse to what little international law there is—as the Clinton administration did in eschewing the term "genocide" in favor of an apparently more passive (but mind-bogglingly inappropriate) "acts of genocide."[3] Likewise, millions of lives would have been saved had we ceased to accept the necessity of preserving state sovereignty as an excuse not to act against regimes brutalizing their people. In short, not only do we need concerted action in the field of humanitarianism, we need fresh, novel, courageous, and determined thinking. Michael Barnett and Thomas

G. Weiss's *Humanitarianism Contested* provides just the perfect place to begin an unfinished journey.

Barnett and Weiss offer the reader one of the most thorough and insightful interventions (no pun intended) into the field of humanitarian action. Given the seriousness with which they have taken the power of language and ideas in their previous scholarly work, individually and collectively, it is no surprise that they should have produced such a superior volume. What is perhaps surprising is that they should have produced an analysis of the paralyses of and possibilities for humanitarianism in such a compelling and pithy fashion and done so in such an accessible and engaging manner.

Barnett and Weiss are both eminent scholars who have combined periods of practice with scholarly endeavors to produce substantial bodies of work that have consistently set the standard. Barnett is University Professor at the George Washington University; and Weiss is Presidential Professor of Political Science at The CUNY Graduate Center and Director of the Ralph Bunche Institute for International Studies. Both have had, and continue to have, illustrious careers, the highlights of which are many. Among other things, Barnett produced one of the most important pieces on the failure of the United Nations to act during the Rwandan genocide.[4] The significance of his work lay not only in the mundane reportage of the "facts of the matter" but also in the seriousness with which he treated the barriers to action put in place by a UN institutional culture and a regime of political possibility. Barnett's work has consistently been among the very best, but it was this book that challenged scholarly and practitioner thinking.

Weiss's work has been similarly at the cutting edge, consistently challenging and provocative and "ahead of the curve." Throughout his intellectual endeavors he has consistently pointed to the role of ideas in shaping international political action, highlighting their capacity to engender change, and pointing to the interests that they often serve. His work on the development of the idea of global governance, as research director of the International Commission on Intervention and State Sovereignty that produced *The Responsibility to Protect*, on the ideational background of the UN, and, more recently, on world government are among his most prominent contributions.[5] We are fortunate enough to include only books in this series on topics and institutions that we believe warrant widespread attention by authors who we know to be serious. A lot of behind-the-scenes work goes into producing the books, by the authors, the production team at Routledge, and Tom Weiss and myself as editors. Very occasionally one of us gets to write a foreword by himself. These occasions, provided only when one of us has a book in the series in which we have acted as author or editor, provide great opportunities to become reacquainted with the work of the other. For me, these are unusually fulfilling moments of pleasure. Barnett and Weiss are at the top of their game. This book promises to go beyond the largely circular debates about humanitarian action, carving out a new space in its wake. It is first-rate and compelling reading—the kind of analysis that should be grasped by all interested in world politics, let alone humanitarian intervention and global institutions.

Rorden Wilkinson, University of Manchester, UK
December 2010

Acknowledgments

One of the pleasant tasks in writing a book is thanking the institutions and people who helped along the way. Our first debt of gratitude goes to the colleagues and contributors to our edited volume *Humanitarianism in Question: Politics, Power, Ethics* published by Cornell University Press in 2008. We have both been involved in the analysis of humanitarian action for some time, individually and collectively, but the learning that occurred during that research and writing endeavor was exceptional. We hope it is not arrogant to state that we believed it desirable and possible to move beyond these essays and write a more succinct and reader-friendly book for a wider audience. Where appropriate, we refer readers to specific chapters in that volume for in-depth analyses of some of the key points to which we refer. In particular, we adapt parts of our own introduction and are grateful for the permission of Cornell University Press.

Each of us has benefited from the support of our home institutions and some of their best graduate students. Most especially, we wish to single out Martin Burke, an advanced student in international relations at the Graduate Center of the City University of New York. Martin's research, analytical, and organizational talents have added value to the content and presentation of this volume as they have to others in this Routledge Global Institutions Series that he so ably manages. As she has done on so many other occasions for books done at the Ralph Bunche Institute for International Studies, Danielle Zach has sharpened the text and made it more readable.

Michael Barnett wishes to thank the University of Minnesota for being such a splendid home over the last number of years, and the Stassen Chair in International Affairs for providing generous financial support.

Finally, we are also extremely grateful that Jan Egeland—the person called "the world's conscience" by *Time* magazine—agreed to grace these pages with his foreword. Jan's commitment and work ethic and basic humanity are in evidence now as the director of the Norwegian Institute for International Studies as they invariably were as the UN's under-secretary-general for humanitarian affairs, secretary-general of the Norwegian Red Cross, and state secretary of the Ministry of Foreign Affairs. His own story about many of the events discussed here can be found in *A Billion Lives: An Eyewitness Report from the Frontlines* (New York: Simon & Schuster, 2008). The world would be a poorer place without this humanitarian.

Notwithstanding the many individuals who helped make this book possible, we alone are responsible for any remaining errors of fact or interpretation.

M. B. and T. G. W.
Washington, DC, and New York
December 2010

Abbreviations

AFSC	American Friends Service Committee
ALNAP	Active Learning Network on Accountability and Performance in Humanitarian Action
BBC	British Broadcasting Corporation
CNN	Cable News Network
CRS	Catholic Relief Service
DRC	Democratic Republic of the Congo
ECHO	European Community Humanitarian Aid Office
ICC	International Criminal Court
ICISS	International Commission on Intervention and State Sovereignty
ICRC	International Committee of the Red Cross
ICVA	International Council of Voluntary Agencies
IDP	internally displaced person
IGO	Intergovernmental organization
IMF	International Monetary Fund
IRC	International Rescue Committee
MSF	Médecins Sans Frontières [Doctors without Borders]
NATO	North Atlantic Treaty Organization
NGO	Nongovernmental organization
OAU	Organization of African Unity
OCHA	Office for the Coordination of Humanitarian Affairs
OECD/DAC	Organization for Economic Co-operation and Development/Development Assistance Committee
Oxfam	Oxford Committee for Famine Relief
R2P	responsibility to protect
UNDP	UN Development Programme
UNHCR	UN High Commissioner for Refugees
UNICEF	UN [International] Children's Fund
UNRRA	United Nations Relief and Rehabilitation Administration
WFP	World Food Programme

Introduction

For the last two decades, humanitarians have careened from pillar to post, from one emergency to another, from euphoria to depression. Aid agencies never anticipated that the end of the Cold War would dampen the demand for their services, but they were hardly prepared for the monumental challenges that they encountered. Some of these horrors became well-covered spectacles. In the early 1990s in Somalia, soldiers landed on beaches under the floodlights of various media while relief workers attempted to save hundreds of thousands of people from conflict-induced famine generated by warlords seeking food aid to feed their ambitions. Around the same time in Bosnia-Herzegovina, aid agencies provided relief to those trapped in so-called safe havens—some of the least safe areas on the planet that the United Nations Security Council had intended to be sanctuaries from Serbian attacks but had failed to provide with enough muscle to prevent atrocities. In Rwanda humanitarian workers were absent during the genocide but began attempting to save hundreds of thousands of displaced peoples in camps militarized and controlled by the architects of the mass murder. In Kosovo, Afghanistan, and Iraq, humanitarian organizations were funded by and operated alongside the invading armies and then were surprised that they were treated as combatants or occupiers by the belligerents. Darfur attracted the attention of many activists, aid agencies, international organizations, and states; but little was done to halt a government whose sitting president was indicted as a war criminal. As death tolls mount, as grandiose proclamations of "never again" go unfulfilled, it is an open question whether humanitarianism is any healthier than the peoples whom it pledges to protect.

Discussions of humanitarian action in the post–Cold War period typically gravitate toward one of two different and not easily reconcilable trends. Some suggest that this is something of a "golden age" of humanitarianism. Although there is no sign that humans are any less cruel, there is some evidence that they are compassionate and willing to act on those feelings. Not only is there a growing willingness of individuals to take risks to help others, but radical improvements in information technology and logistical capacities, when combined with growing international support, make it easier for people to do something in response to acute hardship in distant places. There are more expectations, more promises, and more possibilities for protecting lives at risk, and while they are not fully realized, they have certainly exceeded what was viewed as imaginable a century ago. There is a growing acceptance of the legitimacy of humanitarian action, and its place is firmly entrenched on the global agenda. Funding has skyrocketed. There are more organizations, states, and agencies dedicated to the idea of relieving the needless suffering of afflicted peoples than ever before. There exists a global positioning system that allows relief to be delivered to victims in a matter of hours. An international network exists that can be unleashed when and if summoned.

There is another storyline that sees humanitarianism as entering a new Dark Ages, though the focus here is less on the victims of the world than on the kinds of dilemmas and dangers confronted by those who would help afflicted populations. Philip Gourevitch has ridden the humanitarian roller-coaster for two decades and concludes, "In case after case, a persuasive argument can be made that, over-all, humanitarian aid did as much or even more harm than good.[1] Humanitarians generally believe that being accompanied by or working alongside states and other interested parties hurts their ability to act. Consequently, they covet what they call "humanitarian space," an air pocket that gives them room to breathe in an otherwise suffocating and debris-filled environment—and ensures that they have access to those in need. Yet might there not be times when the only way to save lives involves working with the armed protection of states? Humanitarians pledge to give aid on the basis of need and do not worry as much about the effects of this assistance. But should they provide aid unconditionally? What if doing so means feeding the armies, militias, and killers who clearly benefit from terrorizing civilian populations? At what point should aid workers withdraw either to exert pressure or because conditions are too dangerous? What if aid is no more than a band-aid? Should humanitarianism address the causes of suffering? Even stalwart defenders of humanitarianism concede that the moral necessity of their action is no longer self-evident.[2]

In addition to these and other trying dilemmas, complex emergencies pose more dangers for aid workers than ever before. Humanitarian organizations have been generally ill-equipped for zones of armed conflict where civilian populations are the intended victims, access is difficult, aid workers are in danger of being perceived as threats or as resources to be captured, and everyone's physical safety is in doubt. The standard operating procedures developed between the founding of the International Committee of the Red Cross (ICRC) in 1864 and the collapse of the Berlin Wall provided scant guidance for coming to the rescue in such places as Bosnia, Rwanda, Afghanistan, and Iraq. Improvisation rather than well-honed procedures became the order of the day.

It is now more dangerous to be a civilian aid worker than a military peacekeeper. Etched in the minds of all humanitarians—from bilateral, multilateral, or nongovernmental aid agencies—are the August and September 2003 suicide-bombing attacks on UN headquarters in Baghdad killing 22 followed by another 15 at the ICRC's headquarters; the October 2009 suicide-bombing deaths of five UN officials in Islamabad and the killing of another five UN officials inside their residence in neighboring northern Afghanistan; and the early 2010 murder of six local members of World Vision International in their offices in Islamabad.[3] And as we were sending this manuscript into production, a medical team providing optometry services high in the mountains of northern Afghanistan finished a picnic lunch when Taliban gunmen marched them into the forest and executed seven men and three women. Indeed, by World Humanitarian Day 2010—19 August to commemorate the attack on UN headquarters in Baghdad in 2003—some 700 humanitarian relief workers worldwide had lost their lives trying to aid others.[4] Many aid workers, understandably, seem nostalgic about the supposedly more straightforward emergencies of the past.

The schizophrenic attitude regarding the state of humanitarianism corresponds to an anxious collective identity crisis. What exactly *is* humanitarianism? What are its principles? Can humanitarianism possibly try to do too much? Should it treat symptoms or causes? Should it try to make the world a better place or just a little less horrific? There is no single view on these matters among humanitarians; instead there is constant soul-searching about who they are, what they do, how they do it, and what impact they have. For many, humanitarianism should be a modest endeavor—namely, providing relief to victims of human-made and natural disasters. For others, humanitarianism should not end with the termination of an emergency; just because lives are no longer at immediate risk does not mean that suffering has ended or that other destructive forces will not appear in the future. No longer satisfied with saving individuals today only to have them be in jeopardy tomorrow, many organizations aspire to transform the structural conditions that led to disasters in the first place. There is almost nothing that is not in some humanitarian budget, including economic and social develop-ment, democracy promotion, establishing the rule of law and respect for human rights, and post-conflict peace-building. These ambitious efforts expand the reach of aid workers to help more people in need—but they also mean that humanitarianism cannot help but become part of politics and governance, and even coincide with the grand strategies of powerful states.

The competing storylines regarding whether humanitarianism is experiencing a golden or dark age and ongoing anxieties regarding whether humanitarianism has lost its bearings suggest a two-front battle. One is within the humanitarian community. What is the meaning of humanitarianism? Practitioners and scholars typically treat as the gold standard the ICRC definition—the impartial, neutral, and independent provision of assistance to victims of armed conflicts and natural dis-asters. Although this definition might be the most common, in fact there are many alternatives. Is humanitarianism simply about saving lives at risk, or can it also include trying to alleviate other kinds of suffering, or perhaps even prevent them? Does humanitarianism demand obser-vance of the traditional ICRC principles, or can we imagine that they might actually frustrate the objective of saving the maximum number of lives? How has humanitarianism changed over the decades? Which features have changed? Which have stayed the same? What are the boundaries? Who counts as a member of the humanitarian club and why? Are there certain kinds of actors, namely states, and certain kinds of activities, namely governance, that should be outside the bounds of humanitarianism? Humanitarianism presents itself as beyond politics yet most humanitarians join aid agencies precisely because they want to express their particular brand of politics. What kind of politics should be practiced by humanitarians?

The second battle is between humanitarians and other relevant actors. Humanitarians frequently require the cooperation of those who cause suffering. For example, the ICRC needs the states that are mis-treating prisoners of war to grant access to camps and gulags; and all aid agencies need visas and import licenses from the same authorities who are part of the reason that humanitarians are called upon to help. States are not the only violence-wielding forces that humanitarians must confront. Nonstate actors such as warlords and gangs also pose formidable obstacles to humanitarian operations. For example, operations in Somalia since the 1990s have involved negotiating with a changing set of warlords to have access to civilians. Humanitarians often must compromise with the forces of suffering, both state and nonstate alike; these angels of mercy, in other words, must get their fingernails dirty.

How dirty can they get before they become indistinguishable from those who are causing harm—to the point that they might be causing harm themselves? What if making compromises only creates a compromised world? Or, what if sticking to principles makes humanitarians high-minded to the point of being irrelevant? These and other issues relate not only to the sorts of dilemmas that aid agencies confront in an emergency, but they are related to bigger questions regarding what kind of world humanitarianism wants to and can possibly create.

These battles are closely connected. The attempt by aid agencies to address practical and immediate questions in the field has caused them to wonder about the very definition of humanitarianism. Their existing identities have a dramatic impact on the kinds of missions that they choose to accept and the kinds of dilemmas that they choose to face. In other words, humanitarianism is not only embattled, but its current character is an artifact of ongoing struggles with others and with itself. Although we cannot plot the many ways that these different fronts have affected one other, we must be aware of their relationships.

The story of humanitarianism contested, then, cannot be told without taking into account global forces that are bigger than humanitarianism and the stubborn attempt by fine-minded people to do something. The increased severity and duration of wars have created a growing demand for more and different kinds of action. Globalization and its discontents, as well as ideologies of political economy and evolving discourses of development, have affected where humanitarian organizations go, what they do, and how they are funded. Social movements, motivated by religious and philosophical traditions, remain committed to helping those in need and trying to save the world from itself. In short, humanitarian action is a creature of the world that produces it; and we hope to make that world more understandable by looking through the prism of "humanitarianism contested," the title of this volume. Unlike the English poet Alexander Pope, our subtitle does not question, however, the sanity of those who dare to rush in "where angels fear to tread"; simply we argue that everyone should evaluate the new terrain where humanitarian action takes place.

Any account of the contests engulfing humanitarianism must be attentive to history. This primer provides a history of the present condition of humanitarianism. Current debates have, in fact, been present since the very beginning of humanitarianism. The kinds of ethical dilemmas that currently confront the field are part of a long and distinguished history—even if many observers act as if they are appearing for the first time. The kinds of questions that they ask about themselves and how they should engage the world around them have been first-order questions since the time of humanitarianism's birth. Aid workers confront a world that is constantly changing, which has altered not only the constraints on action but also changed humanitarianism's character.

The end of the Cold War was not the beginning or the end of history, even if that phrase entered into common parlance and although that is the base line for most discussions. Ethical and operational dilemmas are not making their maiden appearances in the last two decades. Humanitarianism has a substantial and meandering history. Today's thorny questions and policy debates should more fully take into consideration this past. Whereas many overviews suggest that the end of the Cold War was ground zero, much of the present can be better understood by excavating the past.

The book is organized to explore these enduring questions and their crucial importance for understanding the humanitarianism of today, yesterday, and tomorrow. Chapter 1 introduces the reader to the basics, beginning with ongoing debates about definitions and identities, and explains why we should care about such a conversation. "Humanitarianism: the essentials," provides a brief overview of the criteria that distinguish humanitarianism, the humanitarian act, and the humanitarian system. It clarifies the three lenses—destruction, production, and salvation—through which readers can peer in order to understand how and why suffering emerges in war zones, and how and why outsiders feel compelled to come to the rescue of others in spite of increasing threats to their own lives. Finally, practitioners and observers routinely claim that the humanitarian sector has significantly expanded over the last 20 years, and we assemble some basic facts and figures against which such claims can be evaluated and which help justify our argument that there have been three distinct historical periods.

These concepts are then applied in the middle four chapters to examine the distinctiveness of what we view as three separate historical periods of humanitarian action from the nineteenth century to the present. Chapters 2 and 3 cover: "'Birth' and maturation, 1864–1945" and "The traditional enterprise, 1945–89." Chapters 4 and 5 discuss the period since 1989 but each with a different focus, the former on "The turbulent post–Cold War era: the 'new' humanitarianism?" and the latter on "Turbulent humanitarianism since 1989: rhetoric meets reality." The contemporary period is the reason that we have written this book, and so the two chapters give us sufficient space to illustrate the terrain where angels fear to tread.

This tripartite chronology allows us to identify broad trends in humanitarian action and to better situate the present in the past, and especially to provide historical, thematic, and demographic overviews.

We integrate the history of humanitarianism with the first chapter's essentials. Chapters 2, 3, 4, and 5 contain numerous historical illustrations, thereby allowing readers to have a better and more specific appreciation of the essential changes that have occurred. They also highlight chilling events that caused humanitarians to lose sleep and wonder about their principles as well as the reality that ethical dilemmas have life-and-death consequences.

Chapter 6, "Humanitarianism's past and possible futures: ten guiding questions," concludes with several themes and trends that dominate the past and also are likely to dominate the future of humanitarianism. While we cannot offer either predictions of what is likely to occur or directives regarding what should occur, we can provide a sense of the choices, trade-offs, and stakes.

1 Humanitarianism
The essentials

- **What *is* humanitarianism?**
- **Driving forces**
- **Three historical periods**
- **The contemporary landscape: growth and increasing violence**
- **Conclusion: embarking on an unfinished journey**

We use the term "essentials" advisedly. There is nothing essential about humanitarianism. By this we do not mean that humanitarianism is a luxury; while it might appear to be for some of those who give, it most certainly is not for those who depend on acts of compassion to survive. Instead, we mean that humanitarianism does not have an essence. Humanitarianism is a work in progress, and its meanings and practices have changed over the years.

In order to underscore the importance of treating as fluid what many analysts and practitioners consider fixed, much of this chapter interrogates the fundamental question: what *is* humanitarianism? Defined by what it aspires to achieve and how it tries to achieve it, such goals and means are surprisingly varied. One way to explore the fault lines and get a sense of what is at stake is by beginning with the "fundamentalist definition"—that is, the definition used by those who Hugo Slim called the "high priests"—and then start relaxing the criteria to see how far we are willing to go before we worry that the meaning of humanitarianism has been stretched beyond the point of recognition. Our goal is not to choose sides (in fact, we ourselves differ) but rather to show the reader how difficult it is to agree on where to draw the line between the acceptable and the unacceptable.

Having identified some fault lines, we speculate briefly about why some definitions have fallen in and out of favor over the decades. Our view is that while battles over the definition of humanitarianism are being waged primarily by practitioners, the context of the debate has been shaped historically by the forces of destruction, production, and salvation. These forces have varied over the decades, helping to create three identifiable periods of humanitarianism and shaping the imperatives of and constraints on humanitarian action within each era. Treating humanitarianism in this way reveals the importance of history and the growth of humanitarian action over the past six decades, and most especially since the end of the Cold War and the discovery of its own HGH—a humanitarianism growth hormone. On this note, we conclude by surveying humanitarianism's current size, scope, and significance.

What *is* humanitarianism?

If there is a high priest of humanitarianism, it is the International Committee of the Red Cross. The oldest of the major humanitarian organizations, and with an official seal of approval by states, for many the ICRC's definition of humanitarianism is the gold standard: the independent, neutral, and impartial provision of relief to victims of armed conflicts and natural disasters. Its goals are modest—to save those at immediate risk of death. In the beginning, it focused on saving the lives of soldiers and reducing their suffering. Decades later it extended assistance to civilians caught in war. Although the ICRC began as a response to human-made disasters, over time it applied its craft to help those affected by natural disasters as well. Hurricanes such as Katrina in August 2005, floods like those of the Indian Ocean tsunami of December 2004 or those in Pakistan during the 2010 monsoon season, and earthquakes such as those in China in 2008 and Haiti in 2010 have been recent showcases for relief. Although it is typical to distinguish them, we must acknowledge that there is a fine line between "natural" and "human-made" disasters. Humans are not responsible for unleashing nature's force, but they do affect the distribution of risk. In Hurricane Katrina the poorer ninth ward was ravaged while some of New Orleans' relatively wealthy neighborhoods escaped the same level of destruction. In January 2010 an earthquake killed nearly 200,000 people in Port-au-Prince, but an earthquake of greater magnitude in the densely populated Santiago, Chile, left only a few hundred dead.

The ICRC's definition focuses not only what humanitarianism is supposed to do, but also how it is supposed to do it. In his famous desiderata, the ICRC's Jean Pictet identified seven defining principles: humanity, impartiality, neutrality, independence, voluntary service, unity, and universality. The first four arguably constitute the core.[1] Humanity commands attention to all people. Impartiality requires that assistance be based on need and not discriminate on the basis of nationality, race, religion, gender, or political opinion. Neutrality demands that humanitarian organizations refrain from taking part in hostilities or from any action that either benefits or disadvantages the parties to an armed conflict. Independence necessitates that assistance not be connected to any of the belligerents or others (especially states) with a stake in the outcome of a war; accordingly, there is a general rule that agencies should either refuse or limit their reliance on government funding, especially from those with interests in the results.

The ICRC derived these principles from years of experience regarding which principles best helped it do its job. In other words, although many humanitarians treat these principles as part of their identity, they also serve important functions. Simply put, they help humanitarians reach people in need. If aid agencies are perceived by combatants as partial, allied with the opposing side, or having a vested interest in the outcome, they will have a difficult time getting access, or even worse, they may become targets. If followed and respected, a "humanitarian space" provides a sanctuary for aid workers and victims. It is important, therefore, that humanitarians be perceived as apolitical, as operating in a world of ethics. Following these principles and being perceived as apolitical are particularly important during times of armed conflict. In sum, humanitarianism is defined as the desire to provide life-saving relief while honoring the principles of humanity, neutrality, impartiality, and independence.

The ICRC and like-minded organizations not only favor this definition, but they resist those actors who depart from it and still claim to be doing humanitarianism. We want to be more agnostic and ask the reader to consider what happens if and when we operate with more relaxed criteria. Doing so is a good analytical exercise. It reveals a set of highly controversial and critical issues regarding contemporary humanitarianism; it more accurately reflects that most aid agencies do not operate according to black-and-white distinctions; and it captures the very real debates among aid agencies regarding what is humanitarianism and who gets to be a member of the club. Again, it is not for us to decide at what point actions that reduce human suffering no longer qualify as humanitarian, but we do insist that any assessment consider the options and understand what is at stake.

What are the goals of humanitarianism? The ICRC limits humanitarianism to the provision of relief to those who are in immediate need. For others, though, humanitarianism does not end with the termination of an emergency; just because lives are no longer at immediate risk does not mean that suffering has ended or that other destructive forces might not appear in the future. Many of today's best-known aid organizations, including CARE, Save the Children, and Oxfam, that do more than provide emergency assistance began as single-minded relief agencies but soon discovered that relief was not enough and began tackling reconstruction and development.

Many organizations now aspire to transform the structural conditions that endanger populations because saving individuals today makes little sense if they are in jeopardy tomorrow—the infamous "well-fed dead."[2] Their work includes development, democracy promotion, establishing the rule of law and respect for human rights, and post-conflict peace-building. Even agencies such as Médecins Sans Frontières (MSF) that focus on medical help in life-threatening emergencies can become political as they respond to the tug to provide long-term care and to alter political and economic arrangements in order to improve access to drugs for the world's poor.

But does this mean that anything that alleviates suffering is an act of humanitarianism? Many state activities, from the provision of welfare support to job training, would then be so characterized. Multinational corporations might claim to be part of the humanitarian sector because of the proposition that international trade leads to economic growth, economic growth leads to increased incomes and tax revenues, increased incomes and tax revenues can translate into improved health care, and improved health care can reduce rates of mortality and morbidity. If humanitarianism means everything, it might very well mean nothing, stretching the concept to the point of uselessness. Not only might it be emptied of meaning, but stretching the concept of humanitarianism to cover an infinite number of activities might, in fact, make it more difficult to succor those who need it during times of need. After all, in order to get access to people, humanitarians have to be trusted. But who will trust someone with such an overarching and ambitious agenda?

According to what principles do humanitarians operate? Assuming that principles are designed to serve a purpose, can we imagine situations where adhering to them becomes positively dysfunctional? The ICRC and some aid agencies tend to abide by core principles regardless of the context. Others, however, make them contingent on their effectiveness in specific situations. Under certain conditions, they might indeed be counter-productive. How can one, for instance, be neutral (or indifferent) in the face of ethnic cleansing and genocide? How does neutrality help the victims of such atrocities? If states are the solution to humanitarian emergencies and are required to end mass killing, then what good is independence? For some, the traditional principles are sacrosanct, in essence defining what humanitarianism is. Humanitarians either commit to them unconditionally, or they are not in the club. The problem, as the veteran humanitarian analyst and practitioner Ian Smillie tells us, is that "the basic elements of so-called 'classical humanitarianism'—neutrality, impartiality and independence—were patchy, weak or simply non-existent."[3]

What is humanitarianism's relationship to politics? Regardless of what they do, nearly all humanitarians like to present themselves as above politics. Remaining apolitical, however, is not always easy and sometimes requires a sleight-of-hand. Even those who insist that they are apolitical nevertheless acknowledge that their actions have political consequences and are often interpreted by those on the ground as deeply political. Moreover, those agencies that aspire to tackle the root causes of conflict and not just its symptoms cannot avoid politics; dealing with symptoms in an emergency is one thing, but rebuilding lives and societies necessitates a direct encounter with politics. Denying politics while trying to promote human rights, democracy, gender empowerment, and fair wages is an exercise in self-delusion. Moreover, humanitarian agencies cannot engage in these activities on their own, and sometimes they are guilty of politics by association. Not only must they broker agreements with political actors, but also they often are financed and aided by states.

Hence, a contrasting perspective holds that it is neither possible nor desirable to separate humanitarianism from politics. Even those aid agencies that explicitly engage in politics are nevertheless cautious regarding their entanglement, fearing that if they cross some imaginary line they will have more difficulty doing their job. Our experience is that humanitarian organizations labor to maintain the illusion that they are separate from politics, but keeping up appearances becomes harder and harder, to the point of being impossible, once they tackle the causes of suffering.

How important are humanitarian motives? Although many readers might find this question slightly asinine, it is a serious concern. We typically think of humanitarians as good people. The label frequently connotes altruistic individuals who give unto others without expecting anything in return, potentially sacrificing something in the process. Although most humanitarian organizations avoid the language of altruism, they stress something of a synonym, voluntarism. Sometimes "voluntary" is translated as "unpaid." The original idea of Henry Dunant, the Swiss businessman responsible for cobbling together a proposal for establishing what would become the International Committee of the Red Cross, was for a relief corps comprised of unpaid volunteers.[4] Yet another interpretation of voluntarism, one that probably better captures its present significance, emphasizes those who willingly accept a dangerous undertaking, who exhibit a certain spirit of selflessness, who are ready to sacrifice for others, and, perhaps most importantly, who are not motivated by economic gain.

Has anyone ever seen a Dunant-type volunteer? In our view, aid workers give to others but are not exempt from expectations of power, esteem, and social status—and are what one veteran called "selfish altruists."[5] They often are exceptional but remain flesh-and-blood human beings with mixed motives and feelings. Furthermore, while few join aid organizations with the expectations of getting rich, the sector has become highly professionalized over the last few decades. And the desire to attract smart people from the private sector and retain highly valued employees has caused aid organizations to worry about competitive salaries, benefit packages, and pensions. Humanitarianism might not be a career like any other, but for many it is increasingly a profession and not an avocation.[6]

The question of whether motives matter, though, goes beyond any assessment of the true motives of aid workers; instead, it concerns whether motives are or should be the measure of success. Do results also not matter? Do outcomes not count? Until the 1990s aid agencies appeared to believe that showing up was enough. But the 1990s reeled off a string of sobering and ultimately morale-busting events that shattered the largely unexamined self-confidence of humanitarian organizations. One big question was whether aid was doing more harm than good. In Somalia, agencies that were giving food to warlords in order to get access to starving populations worried that they were, quite literally, feeding the war machine. The spectacle of aid agencies feeding the perpetrators of the Rwandan genocide in refugee camps alongside their victims presented harsh lessons about intentions and unintended consequences—humanitarian actors are supposed to "do no harm" or at least "minimize the negative effects of their action."[7] In addition to aid agencies' wondering about the results of their actions, donors wanted to know. In some cases they were prepared to withhold funding if they did not get answers, and in other cases were willing to reward those agencies that could answer the tough questions.

The turn to assessing impacts had two results that were largely unforeseen. One was that it was easier said than done. Trying to figure out what works and what does not—especially in emergency settings and even more especially in emergencies in poor, infrastructure-deprived, and violent settings—proved challenging, to say the least. Figuring out which welfare or job-training program works is difficult enough in the United States, and experts disagree all the time; but that is a walk in the park compared to the challenge of trying to understand whether a program designed to educate child soldiers is effective in a war-torn society with limited access and even more limited data. Another implication of trying to measure impact was that it leveled the playing field between non-profit aid agencies and for-profit firms and even militaries.[8] If the bottom line is efficiency and results, then commercial enterprises such as Wal-Mart could count as relief organizations.[9] What if they are more efficient than non-profit organizations and thus save more lives for the buck or euro? Do the recipients of blankets, food, and medicine really care if the money comes from the US government and then is "laundered" through a non-profit agency? Do they really care if life-saving goods are delivered by the US military or a profit-making group like Brown and Root?

Who is a card-carrying humanitarian? Asking whether results matter more than motives complicates how we distinguish humanitarian from other run-of-the-mill organizations that are built for another purpose but might provide relief if so moved. Who gets to be a member? Most people would immediately identify a nongovernmental organization (NGO) from which they have received an appeal in the mail for a contribution—for instance, MSF, CARE, Save the Children, World Vision International, Catholic Relief Services (CRS), or Oxfam. This familiarity owes to their perceived values and general ability to deliver. However, Hugo Slim playfully but perceptively mocks those who claim that humanitarian agencies have a monopoly on relief:

> First, I wonder if there is an analogy between humanitarianism and humour. Laughter is a universal good. What would the world be like if only clowns were allowed to be funny and make people laugh? This would be a terrible world that confined humour to a professional class and restricted a universal human desire and capacity. At times, it can sound as if NGO humanitarians are suggesting something similar about humanitarian action. It is something that they want everyone to value and enjoy but which only they are allowed to do. Often, by implying this, they can come across as smug and self-righteous. If this is what they really think, then this is humanitarian professionalism gone mad.[10]

Slim has a point. Because of their presumed attributes, many intergovernmental organizations—including the World Food Programme (WFP), United Nations Children's Fund (UNICEF), and Office of the United Nations High Commissioner for Refugees (UNHCR)—also are counted by those in the know. The ICRC is the patriarch of the system and is neither nongovernmental nor intergovernmental; in a category of its own, states provide almost all of its resources and also have given it a particular mandate—to develop, protect, and disseminate international humanitarian law—but individual citizens, and not states, are members.

What about charitable and philanthropic foundations that fund and implement programs? For instance, the Bill and Melinda Gates Foundation—already the world's largest foundation before the $30 billion gift from Warren Buffett in 2006—has targeted various life-threatening diseases and now disburses more funds per year than the World Health Organization. It is only the most recent of a long line of philanthropic and charitable organizations, including the Ford, Rockefeller, and Aga Khan foundations, which might be included because of their presumed qualities.

More controversially, what of states and commercial firms, which occasionally provide assistance? For purists, the unequivocal answer is "no." However, if reduction of suffering in disasters is what counts, then more subtlety is required. States can and do contribute directly to relief and thus can save lives; and governments finance the bulk of relief budgets and of course virtually the entire budgets of UN and other intergovernmental organizations. Since 1990 the business community has provided significant financial support, delivered relief, and encouraged others to contribute to the cause. Non-profit agencies will grudgingly acknowledge the contributions of states and commercial firms; but because their motives are wrong, they are not humanitarian organizations. States and commercial firms have ulterior motives when they deliver relief: states generally get involved when their foreign policy interests are at stake, and the private sector recognizes that being seen as doing good can also be good for business. Does any of this really matter?

Existing humanitarian agencies that stress motives and principles rather than outcomes in order to take the high road have to wonder how distant they are from the low road. Although for-profit relief enterprises are largely driven by contracts and not by perceived needs, even not-for-profit agencies also are obliged to recognize economic imperatives; and financial concerns shape their decisions and activities. Moreover, we should not be so ready to assume that non-profits necessarily have purer and nobler motives than for-profit firms; there is plenty of evidence that staff have mixed motives everywhere.

As we repeatedly stress, there are more shades of gray than either black or white—certainly much more than many humanitarians are prepared to acknowledge. While venerable aid agencies use traditional principles to delimit their activities, definitional boundaries are rather porous.

Moreover, there is considerable diversity within the humanitarian sector and even within individual agencies. There are agencies that focus on emergency relief during times of war and others that seek to provide long-term empowerment. Over the last decade various practitioners and scholars have offered a range of classifications and taxonomies that are intended to define critical differences among agencies. Some criteria include big versus small, secular versus religious, European versus American, and full-service versus relief-oriented. The claim, in other words, is that these differences in nationalities, mandates, organizational cultures, and size are relevant for understanding what humanitarian organizations do, how they react to circumstances, and how they respond to external pressures.[11]

Finally, criteria and their relative weights are generally defined by those working within the sector. Although there might be principled reasons why existing humanitarian organizations want to preserve existing distinctions, there are also self-interested reasons why they have a stake in keeping membership limited and their trademarks copyrighted, including the desire to maintain their autonomy and resource base.

Is humanitarianism universal? Previous questions about humanitarianism suggest a challenge to its purported universality. Although the idea of saving lives and relieving suffering is hardly a Western or Christian creation, modern humanitarianism's origins are anchored in Western history and Christian thought. Consequently, tensions have always existed between the presumed universality of aid agencies and their Western roots. Humanitarians frequently used their goals and principles as evidence of their universal orientation and appeal. They aspired to save lives regardless of nationalities, religions, cultures, or other identity markers. Their traditional principles underscored their depoliticized and universal character.

However, the claim to universality was never as stable and crystalline as partisans imagined; it was invariably challenged by countervailing forces who viewed universal claims as a move by the wealthy and powerful to impose their worldviews on the weak and vulnerable. Such challenges have become more acute and frequent as aid agencies have become more closely linked to Western states and committed to a politics of transformation that diffuses and protects values associated with the West. What were mild and low-decibel grumblings in the Balkans became far harsher and louder in Iraq and Afghanistan. The critique of universalism represents a mortal threat to humanitarianism's identity.

So, once again we ask, what *is* humanitarianism? The ongoing debate reveals a struggle to redefine its identity. Some prefer a narrow, fastidious definition of the sort associated with the ICRC rather than an expansive, slippery one. Others, however, maintain that placing the bar too high means potentially foregoing many activities that might otherwise save lives and relieve suffering; and consequently, they want to operate with a more relaxed set of criteria. Doing so, however, might very well open the floodgates to all kinds of fly-by-night, ambulance-chasing, opportunistic, and media-seeking individuals and institutions that are more motivated by the appearance of doing good rather than actually doing good.

What is at stake is more than simply who is admitted as a member of the club. Humanitarianism concerns saving lives at risk. In emergencies, it involves setting up feeding stations, providing medical facilities, delivering food, building shelters, and protecting the rights of vulnerable populations. After the end of the emergency phase, shattered lives need to be repaired and reconstructed, local societies' wounds healed. The challenge evolves from keeping individuals alive to creating conditions that enable victims to survive and thrive on their own. Aid workers often undergo considerable hardship and run considerable risks to help those in need. Sometimes their only protection in war zones is the respect that they are conferred by combatants because of the presumption that they are only there to keep people alive.[12] The goals, principles, and relationships to politics are not merely rhetorical flourishes to be buried in documents in filing cabinets or to display on brochures and websites. Rather, such expressions of identity govern the means and ends of humanitarian action as well as shape the most effective ways to establish lifelines to vulnerable populations.

Driving forces

What creates and constrains humanitarianism? The answer to both questions resides outside of humanitarianism or, more precisely, highlights the extent to which humanitarianism exists in this world. As we have already suggested, humanitarians cannot go where they want when they want—they are limited by time, resources, and support; and they must negotiate access with sovereign-sensitive states and power-hungry nonstate actors who often care more about their immediate political objectives than they do about the lives of innocents. There thus are very real constraints. But the world does more than constrain humanitarianism—it also helps to shape what it is. Resembling the debate over whether the human identity is a product of nature or nurture, the humanitarian identity is a product of both. Whose suffering matters, what they need to alleviate their suffering, and what humans are rumored to require to achieve their humanity are shaped by the life and times in which humanitarianism exists. Even the ICRC, which operates with a minimal definition of humanitarianism, nevertheless has expanded its sense of compassion from the exclusive focus on soldiers during wartime to civilians at risk because of human-made emergencies and natural disasters. Although it is possible to see this extension as a natural outgrowth, our view is that nature has less to do with it than does the environment in which the ICRC and other humanitarian agencies have evolved.

We require a better understanding of how the global environment creates and constrains humanitarianism. Below we identify three forces of humanitarianism: destruction, production, and salvation.[13]

The forces of destruction

The forces of destruction are the most obvious causes of misery and targets for attention by an analytical cottage industry of specialists in international peace and security. They include acts of violence that place individuals at immediate risk. Massacres, international and civil wars, war crimes, crimes against humanity, and war-induced famines have typically served to trumpet the "call to alms."[14] Changes in military technology and strategy simultaneously made destruction easier and fostered the desire to expand the laws of war and provide more protection and emergency assistance to civilians.

Acts of violence, though, would not necessarily lead to international humanitarian action were it not for their visibility. Media imagery—beginning with war-reporting in the mid-nineteenth century and continuing with contemporary satellite, telecommunications, and web-based technologies—has increased public awareness. In turn, such coverage has sometimes created a demand that something be done in the face of conscience-shocking suffering. States do not always wait for their citizens to demand action; at times they decide that their security interests might be furthered by humanitarian action. States tend to become most pained when suffering intersects with their already existing security interests, and they are not averse to legitimating their foreign policy actions by flying the flag of humanitarianism.

The forces of production

Unlike destruction, which has customarily been an integral component of humanitarian analyses, the forces of production have not. They include capitalism and the global economy, ideologies regarding the state's role in society, and the funding environment. The debate regarding the relationship between capitalism and humanitarianism emerged when formal organizations appeared in the early nineteenth century and declared that they were trying to save the world from itself.

One line of thought treats capitalism as the structure and humanitarianism as part of the superstructure that is functionally valuable for capitalist reproduction and expansion. In the *Communist Manifesto*, Karl Marx identified "economists, philanthropists, humanitarians, improvers of the condition of the working class, organizers of charity, members of society for the prevention of cruelty to animals, temperance fanatics, hold-and-corner reformers of every imaginable kind" as operating to smooth over social grievances and help improve bourgeois society.[15] Similarly, some accounts of the end of slavery treat the abolitionists as closet capitalists, or as pushing on an open door because slavery was no longer economically viable and new forms of labor relations were desirable given changes in the agrarian economy and industrialization.[16]

An alternative view does not reduce humanitarianism to the functional needs of capital but instead traces how dislocations caused by market forces laid the groundwork for humanitarianism. Market expansion, industrialization, and urbanization undermined existing normative orders. In response, religious and secular leaders proposed solutions that included new kinds of public help that would restore moral order and that could also further capitalism. For instance, when industrialists saw rampant alcohol consumption as a major problem for productivity, they supported temperance movements that encouraged individuals to become sober, self-disciplined, and responsible.[17]

Something of a similar debate surrounds the contemporary relationship between economic forces and moral action. Some suggest that the when, where, and why of humanitarian action can be reduced to mere economic imperatives. Formerly a charge that was leveled mainly at states, NGO activities more recently have been coupled to the needs of capitalist expansion and stabilization. Post-conflict stabilization programs include, for instance, market-oriented development. Throughout many societies in the developing world, a stripped-down state pursuing structural adjustment programs is increasingly obliged to call upon outside humanitarian organizations to provide basic social services. Aid agencies, in short, are becoming welfare workers as the neoliberal state outsources its basic welfare functions while focusing on the needs of the private sector. Fiona Terry warns: "If aid organizations pursue conflict resolution and peace-building activities, they are likely not only to increase the negative consequences of humanitarian action, but to further exonerate states of their responsibilities in these realms."[18]

Ideologies regarding the state's proper role have also shaped the demands for humanitarian assistance. During the nineteenth century's era of Dickensian capitalism in Europe, various charitable organizations stepped in when the state failed. Meanwhile in the United States, the combination of a growing urban underclass alongside oil and manufacturing tycoons led the latter to create and support various kinds of charitable organizations to improve human welfare.[19] The emergence of the welfare state after the 1930s increased the resources available for such activities. The post-1980s ideology of neoliberalism and the limited state created an even greater demand for humanitarian organizations as well as an accompanying boost for the justifications about relying more upon private and less upon governmental agencies.

The discourses of globalization have shaped the professionalization, bureaucratization, and rationalization of the humanitarian "firm." Indeed, "the formal system has adopted many of the routine practices of modern welfare provision in Western states," Hugo Slim observes. "To this end, it has tried to adopt a modern bureaucratic model of management and organization to shape and sharpen its fast-growing organizations whose smaller antecedents were originally based on simpler notions of charity, volunteerism, activism, and social service."[20] Moreover, Western governments have turned to NGOs because they were supposedly more efficient in delivering services than public organizations, either bilateral or intergovernmental.[21]

No discourse is value neutral and certainly not the humanitarian one. Stephen Hopgood vividly observes that language has changed substantially: humanitarian organizations speak of "beneficiaries," have offices that cultivate "clients," make use of their "brand," aspire to increase their "efficiency," and adopt modern "accountability" and governance mechanisms.[22] Furthermore, as Janice Stein notes, understandings of accountability imported directly from the business world usually privilege the donor over the recipient.[23] A heightened emphasis on efficiency and the search for objective indicators of success might lead to eliminating goals that are tough to quantify, such as the desire to restore dignity to victimized populations and to create a genuine cosmopolitanism.

The funding environment obviously shapes humanitarian action. Money is scarce while populations in need are not. During well-publicized disasters, humanitarian organizations are often flush, but common is the anguish about maintaining the funding base when media attention wanes. Appeals must tug on heartstrings and convince viewers and readers that they can make a difference. Some donors ask for little or nothing in return. Such faith-based organizations as World Vision

International, the American Friends Service Committee (AFSC), and Lutheran World Relief depend on religious constituencies and thus can count on core funds with few preconditions.

Agencies that rely on official funding, however, are less fortunate because they must manage relations with finicky, temperamental, and demanding governments whose officials and parliaments expect to exert control over how funds are used. In the 1990s the amount of funding available for humanitarian activities nearly tripled, but increasingly these resources came from a handful of powerful states, were earmarked, and were accompanied by greater controls and conditions to try and ensure that donors got something for their money—the well known relationship between the payer, the piper, and the tune. Organizations like the International Rescue Committee (IRC) and CARE found themselves dedicating more and more time at their board meetings to the problem of trying to maintain a high public profile in order to manage their relations with the US government, from which they received the bulk of their funding.

Competition for scarce resources is an essential feature of the funding environment. Competition can encourage agencies to become more effective at existing tasks; to specialize in different areas, such as sanitation, shelter, and medicine; to compete for market share by expanding into new areas such as democracy promotion and peace-building; to stress public relations and attempt to develop and protect their brand; to move into high-profile areas such as advocacy and de-emphasize less captivating areas such as building latrines that nevertheless might save more lives. Also, pressure may arise to alter principles, priorities, and policies so that they are more consistent with the demands of funders. Such countervailing pressures are present in every high-profile emergency and often in less visible ones as well.

The forces of salvation

In analytical if not motivational terms, the forces of salvation have been remarkably underplayed. They consist of moral discourses, religious beliefs, ethical commitments, and international norms to help distant strangers. Such imperatives are, of course, as old as humankind. Yet in the nineteenth century, ethical commitments began to be institutionalized and internationalized. The Enlightenment and Christian reform movements in Europe helped to foster the discourse of humanity and the rights-bearing individual, to overlook superficial differences in favor of a broad community of humankind, and to create a faith in the possibility of using social institutions to bring progress to society and perfect the individual.[24] The institutionalization of liberalism—emphasizing freedom, progress, development, individual autonomy, and liberty—historically translated into support for democracy, markets, human rights, and the rule of law. In turn, the dominance of liberalism in the humanitarian sector is linked to the possibility of engineering a peaceful and productive society.

Religious beliefs also contribute to a humanitarian ethic. Charity is a longstanding religious value. Christianity's notion of love and compassion includes obligations to strangers.[25] *Zakat*, which roughly translates to voluntarism, is one of the five pillars of Islam and reflects Islamic identity, commands various forms of charity, and is intended to foster solidarity within the community.[26] *Tzadakah* and the idea of repairing the world make charity and good works part of the Jewish identity.[27] In older spiritual traditions, service to and solidarity with others go beyond injunction and are living values or principles emanating from the supreme wisdom of the inherent unity and interdependence of all life and creation. The millennial Hindu philosophy of the *Upanishads* declares, "Wisdom means a life of selfless service," because the wise "realize that all life is one" and "are at home everywhere and see themselves in all beings."[28] The southern African concept of *ubuntu* popularized by Archbishop Desmond Tutu underlines the fundamental interdependence that renders solidarity with and protection of the other instinctual and natural.[29] In brief, tremendous historical and cross-cultural variations exist regarding whether faith demands a missionary impulse and whether charity extends to those outside the community of the faithful; but many religions hold that charity is a cornerstone of religious identity.[30]

Yet arguably it is Christianity and Christian faith-based organizations that so far have had the most significant influence on contemporary humanitarian action. They were present at the creation—usually dated to the nineteenth century. The various "awakenings" fed into new kinds of social reform movements: Quakers and Protestants helped to spearhead abolitionism; various missionaries were at the forefront of trying to improve the lives of those at home and of the colonized; and faith-based organizations were prominent in delivering relief to victims of war and natural disasters. The "just war tradition" has found its way into norms and principles including, most recently, the responsibility to protect.[31] The image of the Good Samaritan is widespread throughout the humanitarian industry.[32] Among the top contributors to international assistance are such religion-inspired NGOs as World Vision, Catholic Relief Services, Lutheran World Relief, and Adventist Development and Relief Agency. While relatively modest in resources, the Christian pacifists play a disproportionate role through the AFSC (Quakers), the Mennonite Central Committee, and the Unitarian-Universalist Service Committee. While many have distanced themselves from their proselytizing origins and are fairly secular in their activities, much of the current criticism of Western aid agencies centers around the limitations of their Judeo-Christian cultural bias among what are increasingly Muslim clients.

Also important are international laws, norms, and principles. The meaning of sovereignty has varied from one historical era to another, and these variations matter greatly for what humanitarian actors can and therefore should do. During the period of European imperial domination, humanitarian action by colonial states and missionaries was frequently presented as helping to create self-governing and civilized states that could become independent and sovereign. Over the last two decades, a shift has occurred away from a view that the state possesses absolute sovereignty and toward one in which citizens too are sovereign. States are increasingly perceived as having obligations to their citizens. According to the responsibility to protect doctrine, when states are either unable or unwilling to fulfill these obligations, they forfeit their sovereignty to the international community of other states.[33] The discourse of human rights has also shaped the demand for various kinds of interventions that were presumed to help protect individuals from abuse and to give them the opportunities and capabilities to improve their lives.[34]

In general, the discourses surrounding rights, sovereignty, and justice have slowly but impressively created new standards of expectations for states. In particular, they have provided new standards of civilization and new rhetoric to justify intervention on behalf of the weak and powerless. These developments, as we see in Chapter 4, have been contested and resisted.

Three historical periods

Drawing lines between historical periods is always subjective and even slightly arbitrary. However, we use three that provide the structure for the middle chapters of this book: 1859 to 1945; 1945 to 1989; and 1989 to the present.

During the 1859 battle of Solferino, Henry Dunant witnessed what happens when soldiers are treated as disposable, and pledged to do something about it. Out of misplaced respect for tradition, we also begin the story here. However, in many respects this sense of history is both out of date and a convenience for the ICRC and others who prefer their humanitarianism to flow from the Dunantist tradition.

Specifically, as Barnett argues elsewhere, modern humanitarianism had its origins in transformations that were occurring in the late eighteenth and early nineteenth centuries, especially visible in the abolitionist movement.[35] For abolitionists the issue was not about saving lives at immediate risk because of warfare but rather alleviating unnecessary suffering caused by slavery. Although we do not discuss this history, which has been well covered elsewhere, this tradition is most clearly connected to that view of humanitarianism that is comfortable delving into the causes of suffering.

Our decision to speed past World War I and mark the end of the first period with the end of World War II is slightly unconventional but quite justifiable. Except for the ICRC and a handful of NGOs that emerged in response to World War I, there were very few permanent organizations. Instead, most came and went with an emergency—until World War II, when a new generation of aid agencies came into existence in Europe and then developed a global reach. Their permanence introduced an entirely new set of dynamics, including a growing consideration of the purpose of humanitarianism, its proper relationship to states, and the principles guiding actions in the field. In short, we argue that there is a continuity from the establishment of the ICRC in 1863 until the end of World War II.

We have already suggested some of the ways in which the post–World War II period differs from what came before, but two dimensions should be highlighted. One is that the existence of multiple humanitarianisms became more evident as various agencies such as the CRS and CARE began to create development programs alongside their emergency relief capacity, distinguishing them from the ICRC and a handful of other medical emergency organizations, such as MSF. At this point there was no explicit debate over the meaning of humanitarianism because those agencies that delivered relief plus something else were content to leave the "humanitarian" label for others. Except during times of war, there was no reason to wage a terminological battle precisely because these different camps rarely had to interact in the field. This leads to the second point of difference: numerous aid agencies, and not only the ICRC, began delivering aid during active armed conflicts. This was not the first time that aid agencies had to mix with contending troops, but they were doing so with greater frequency and with irregular forces that had no formal relationship to international humanitarian law. The consequence was that in places such as Biafra, Vietnam, Cambodia, and Ethiopia aid agencies were forced to navigate through and negotiate with national governments, rebel forces, and great and regional powers that had vested interests in the outcomes of specific armed conflicts.

The last period begins with the end of the Cold War and continues today. In many respects the tensions, dilemmas, and trends that we see in the previous periods continue; in other words, we emphasize how the contemporary period is embedded in humanitarian history and how developments that observers treat as new are in fact as old as humanitarianism itself. Although we deny the proposition that the post–Cold War era is new, it exhibits enough distinctiveness to warrant being treated as a separate period. The sheer explosion of aid agencies in all manner of relief and reconstruction is one characteristic; and this growing population of actors taking on more than ever has injected an urgency into the kinds of questions that we raised earlier in the chapter. This urgency is especially evident when humanitarianism has gotten too big for its own good, which in turn raises the possibility that it should look more carefully before leaping into the arms of states and into the world of politics. In other words, if humanitarians are arguing about first principles and undergoing something of an identity crisis, it is not only because they are more aware than ever before; but also there are more pressures than ever before. To give the reader a better sense of what has taken place over the last two decades, we now consider some markers of the sector's growth.

The contemporary landscape: growth and increasing violence

Worldwide turbulence over the last two decades appears to have dramatically increased the scope, scale, and significance of humanitarian action. We utter three words of caution before supporting such a generalization with facts and figures.

The first is that other historical periods might well compare with the current moment—not in terms of absolute size and scale or the technological capacity to reach affected populations but certainly in terms of ambitions, constraints on access, and threats to personnel. Said otherwise, too many contemporary accounts proceed as if humanitarianism began with the end of the Cold War, thereby demonstrating an absence of historical memory and restricting the basis for meaningful comparisons. For instance, a conversation about the "uniqueness" of Rwanda's militarized refugee camps conveniently forgets experiences in El Salvador, Lebanon, Cambodia, and Pakistan in the 1970s and 1980s. Those expressing shock about being too closely identified with belligerents in Somalia in the early 1990s after the end of the Cold War overlook positions previously taken by humanitarians in Vietnam, Biafra, and Nicaragua during the Cold War. Those hinting that only recently have aid agencies had to weigh the value of neutrality and independence ignore the extent to which debates about their downsides accompanied the Holocaust of World War II and the Vietnamese intervention in Cambodia in 1978.

The second qualification reflects the absence of longitudinal data on basic categories such as expenditure, income, number of organizations, and activities. James Fearon provides a list of various ways to measure increases in emergency relief. Among the reasons that explain the paucity of data include: agencies and the military are often not forthcoming; reporting periods vary; disbursements and commitments are not always distinguished; beneficiaries are hard to count; and the absence of common reporting requirements even among Western donor countries of the Organisation for Economic Co-operation and Development (OECD). Also, prior to the 1980s, very few aid organizations documented changing mission statements, sources of income, how and where they spent funds, and relationships with international and local partners. Moreover, the accuracy of available data is doubtful in light of little standardization and too few common definitions. In addition, institutional memory is hardly fostered with high staff turnover—for example, in recent years 25 percent for the Red Cross Movement; 35 percent for CARE; and 50 percent for MSF. Many figures are anecdotal, but a recent comparison shows that the average duration of an expatriate mission for MSF is 5.2 months as compared to the ICRC's 10.1 months.[36]

The third word of caution regards what is *not* counted as part of the worldwide humanitarian response. Neighbors and neighboring areas or countries often provide support or harbor people who have fled wars, but such help is rarely recorded. Friends and family members living outside the war zone may send remittances, but such help is private and thus not subject to international accounting. Both the private sector and the military—from the affected area as well as from outside it—give humanitarian aid; but unless they are channeled through NGOs or reported to the UN's Financial Tracking System, many such contributions are likely to be overlooked. Also, there is a fair bit of private religious giving that does not go through the "system." For instance, there are more mega-churches than ever before with their own missionary and social action arms that are deeply involved in development, and when emergency strikes they have the opportunity to give directly to affected communities rather than going through established NGOs or the United Nations.

More actors, more activities

Notwithstanding these caveats, there nonetheless is evidence that the humanitarian sector has undergone significant change since the end of the Cold War—most noticeably in its density, resources, and activities. To start, the sheer growth in organizational numbers is striking.[37] Notwithstanding debate about who is and who is not a humanitarian organization, presently there are at least 2,500 NGOs in the business, but only about 260 are really serious players.[38] In fact in 2001, the half-a-dozen or so of the largest NGOs controlled between $2.5 billion and $3 billion, or about half of all global humanitarian assistance.[39] These figures exclude those NGOs not engaged in relief or the mom-and-pop organizations that inevitably flock to emergencies. In fact, MSF's expenditures in 2007 were larger than Saudi Arabia's, while those of World Vision and Caritas outstripped all but four DAC donor countries.[40]

Although we do not have global longitudinal data, a detailed survey of US-based private voluntary agencies engaged in relief and development finds that considerable growth has taken place over the last three-quarters of a century. In 1940, shortly after the start of World War II, the number of US-based organizations rose to 387 (from 240), but the numbers dropped to 103 in 1946 and 60 in 1948. They rose steadily thereafter and reached 543 in 2005. The growth was especially dramatic from 1986 to 1994 when the number increased from 178 to 506.[41]

Not only has the total number increased but so too have the funds and market share of the very largest among them. Dramatic crises account for spikes in specific emergencies. For instance, over 200 international NGOs were reported on the ground in Sarajevo and Kigali. The numbers of people working in the NGO sector grew by 91 percent from 1997 to 2005, while overall the international humanitarian system (if the UN system and the ICRC are also included) experienced a 77 percent surge in personnel.[42]

How many humanitarian aid workers are there worldwide? While Stoddard and her colleagues hazard a guess of over 200,000, in a major new study on the scope of the enterprise, Peter Walker and Catherine Russ confess: "We have no idea what size this population is." Estimates include everyone from cleaning personnel and drivers in field offices to CEOs in headquarters. As a result of vague and inconsistent definitions and poor reporting, Walker and Russ extrapolate from solid Oxfam data and estimate that there are some 30,000 humanitarian professionals (both local and expatriate) worldwide.[43]

These totals undoubtedly underestimate the growth trend because we can only easily count those based in the West. While resources and institutions mainly come from industrialized countries, an active relief sector exists in the non-Western world, most obviously in Islamic countries. About half of war victims since the 1990s have been Muslim. Hence, it is unfortunate that speculation and salacious accounts trump the search for knowledge and insights since September 11; rather than research about humanitarian efforts, most attention is directed at the putative connections between Islamic charitable organizations and terrorism,[44] and more especially diasporas.[45]

Intergovernmental organizations are prominent in the sector. The UNHCR and other intergovernmental agencies were born as humanitarians. Others were created decades ago to foster development but are increasingly involved in relief and reconstruction because of available resources, including the United Nations Development Programme (UNDP) and the World Bank, both of which have moved steadily upstream toward the eye of the humanitarian storm rather than single mindedly pursuing their focus on development. Similarly UN specialized agencies—for example, the World Health Organization and the UN Educational, Scientific and Cultural Organization—until recently had virtually non-existent disaster programs but have expanded to meet the new demand and availability of funding. Consequently, institutions that might not have counted as humanitarian in the 1980s are today.

There has also been a growth in the number of international and regional organizations whose primary responsibility is coordination, including the European Community Humanitarian Aid Office (ECHO), the UN's Inter-Agency Standing Committee, and the Office for the Coordination of Humanitarian Affairs (preceded by the Department of Humanitarian Affairs). The same phenomenon exists for NGOs in the United States and Europe, including InterAction in Washington, DC; the International Council for Voluntary Action (ICVA) and Emergency Committee for Humanitarian Response in Geneva; and Voluntary Organisations in Cooperation in Emergencies in Brussels.

As hinted earlier, there has also been a dramatic expansion of the activities associated with humanitarianism. Organizations that were once dedicated to relief expanded into other domains; and organizations that had a dual mandate (i.e., relief and development) but never really considered the relationship between relief and non-relief goals were obliged to do so. Institutions are moving both "upstream" (toward helping in the midst of war) and "downstream" (toward post-conflict peace-building and ultimately development), which means few UN organizations or NGOs do not carry the mantle of broad-brush humanitarianism.

Furthermore, states, for-profit disaster firms, and other businesses, as well as various foundations, are increasingly prominent contributors to humanitarian action. While the West continues to dominate the numbers, more and more governments are responding to disasters of all sorts. For example, whereas 16 states pledged their support to Bosnia in the mid-1990s, most from the West, a more diverse group of 73 attended the 2003 pledging conference in Madrid for Iraq, and an unprecedented 92 responded to the December 2004 Indian Ocean tsunami. One recent overview summarized, "From as few as a dozen government financiers just over a decade ago, it is now commonplace to see 50 or 60 donor governments supporting a humanitarian response."[46]

Such important non-Western donors as China, Saudi Arabia, and India have accounted for up to 12 percent of official humanitarian assistance in a given year; and their influence in certain crises—for example, Afghanistan or Palestine—is obviously far more significant. Indeed, most of the countries that are not members of the OECD's Development Assistance Committee (DAC) concentrate their aid on neighboring countries; and the vast bulk of such assistance (over 90 percent or almost $1 billion in 2008) emanates from the Gulf states. In fact, Saudia Arabia accounted for three quarters of the non-OECD/DAC sum and was the third largest humanitarian donor in the world that year.[47] Along with the United Arab Emirates and Kuwait, these states now account for larger humanitarian expenditures than some smaller Western countries.

As noted earlier, we know precious little about whether non-traditional donors follow the major Western states in their rationales for aid inter-ventions, their prioritization for policy options, or their choice for response channels.[48] But they resemble their OECD counterparts in sharing a preference for bilateral aid to countries in their regions, which suggests that they too are using their financial support as a political tool to increase their influence. Nonetheless, the international system remains essentially a North American and Western European enterprise, account-ing for about $11 billion of the total of just over $12 billion of official humanitarian assistance in 2008.[49] In short, "It works wherever it can in international society but is not really owned by all of international society."[50]

Purses and purse strings

There are increasing financial resources available for the industry. Private contributions have increased, but most impressive has been the growth in official (i.e., governmental) assistance. Between 1990 and 2000 aid levels rose nearly threefold, from $2.1 billion to $5.9 billion—and in 2005/6 amounted to over $10 billion.[51] In the last year for which data are available, 2008, the best "guesstimate" was a total of some $18 bil-lion, up about $3 billion from the previous year.[52] To put this in some historical context as we catch our breath, in 1967 just before the Nigerian civil war, the ICRC's annual budget was only half a million dollars; a year later it was spending three times that much each month in Biafra; and in 2010 the annual budget was over $1 billion.

Considerable debate surrounds whether humanitarian assistance (defined as short-term, life-saving, and exceptional) is growing at the expense of development assistance. As *Global Humanitarian Assistance 2009* points out, "the majority of humanitarian assistance over the past 13 years has been spent on long-term, protracted crises in countries that are classified as 'chronically poor.'"[53] In fact, some $3 billion of the total $18 billion in 2008 were reported as post-conflict and security-related expenditures. Humanitarian and development assistance are growing closer together, or perhaps such distinctions are irrelevant in a large number of cases.

Moreover, as a percentage of official development assistance (ODA), humanitarian aid rose from an average of 5.83 percent between 1989 and 1993 to 10.5 percent in 2000.[54] Over a longer period, total ODA has shrunk, but the humanitarian component has continued to grow. "From 1970–90 humanitarian aid was less than 3% of total ODA," calculated a team from the Overseas Development Institute. "While ODA ... as a whole has been declining as a share of donor countries' national wealth or Gross National Income (GNI), humanitarian ODA has been growing. In 1970 DAC member countries gave 0.4 of a cent in humanitarian aid for every $100 in national income. In 2001 it was 2.3 cents."[55]

In spite of its miserly performance at the bottom of the OECD's per capita ODA scale, the United States is the lead country donor by a factor of three; in 1999, for instance, its humanitarian outlays exceeded the total assistance of the next 12 largest Western donor countries. Between 1995 and 1997, Washington provided 20 percent of total humanitarian assistance, and then in the following three years its contribution rose to 30 percent. The second largest donor is the European Union, followed by the United Kingdom and several other European countries; indeed, the EU and European countries together now account for 50 percent of aid totals worldwide, and probably a similar portion of humanitarian assistance totals. Canada and Japan are also important sources.

Conditions and strings on how aid may be used have accompanied the increases. Multilateral aid is technically defined as that channeled through intergovernmental organizations, which supposedly have discretion over how the money is spent—although it would be naïve to think that UN organizations would disregard the expressed preferences of major member states or that ECHO would turn a deaf ear to its major European member states. Even the threat to apply bilateral aid leverage can mean that a particular donor country dictates either to a multilateral organization how money should be spent or how it should be sub-contracted to non-multilateral organizations such as NGOs. Earmarking is when the donor dictates where and how assistance may be used, frequently identifying regions, countries, operations, or even projects; this approach is especially prominent if a government has geopolitical interests to protect or domestic constituencies to satisfy.

Since the 1980s there has been a shift away from multilateral toward bilateral aid and increased earmarking.[56] In 1988 states directed roughly 45 percent of humanitarian assistance through UN agencies. After 1994, however, the average dropped to 25 percent (and even lower in 1999 because of Kosovo).[57] A decade later the trend continued downward toward 11 percent, with only some $913 million of totally un-earmarked multilateral funds of the total of $8.7 billion in 2007's humanitarian expenditures.[58]

What explains this shift? It could be that states no longer trust the judgment of multilateral aid agencies and want to play a greater role. More likely, though, is that state interests are at work. For instance, of the top 50 recipients of bilateral assistance between 1996 and 1999, the states of the former Yugoslavia, Israel/Palestine, and Iraq received 50 percent of the available resources.[59] In 2002 the impact of 9/11 already was obvious as nearly half of all funds given by donor governments to the UN's 25 appeals for assistance went to Afghanistan.[60] As we saw earlier, there is little difference between Western and non-OECD donors when it comes to the preference of bilateral over multilateral channels; the geopolitical calculations of donors essentially trump basic humanitarian values.

If funding decisions were based solely on need, then places such as Sudan, the Democratic Republic of the Congo (DRC), northern Uganda, and Angola would leapfrog to the top of the list. When wars were raging in the Balkans, for example, in per capita terms it was 10–20 times better to be a war victim there than in Africa. Otherwise said, from 1993 to 2000 almost half of the funds from ECHO were disbursed in Europe. In that same year, consolidated appeals generated about $10 per capita for North Korea or Uganda but $185 for Southeastern Europe.[61] In general, while non-Western donors have entered the market with more aid than ever before, the vast bulk of resources were still controlled by a few countries that were more inclined to impose conditions and channel aid toward their priorities rather than human needs. An intri-guing anomaly is that donors are nonetheless channeling increasing portions of their multilateral funds through financing mechanisms such as the UN's Central Emergency Response Fund, "which helps to ensure more equitable funding between crises, and the country-level pooled mechanisms, which are designed to ensure that priority needs are met within specific crises."[62] Although practice suggests that politics trump ethics, the principles still privilege aid based on need.

If state interests are and have always been in the driver's seat, then perhaps the trend toward bilateralism and earmarking is only a change in how states make sure that aid serves their interests. Maybe states are simply being less covert. "With the end of the Cold War, with the increased involvement of Western troops in distant complex emergencies," Ian Smillie contends, "it could be argued that the reassertion of direct forms of political control over humanitarian action has become more evident, and perhaps more profound."[63]

Risky business

Finally, their growing presence in violent environments means that the current moment can also be distinguished from earlier ones by the risks to aid workers.[64] In the last decade over 200 civilian UN staff (that is, not including military peacekeepers whose fatalities have been fewer) were killed in almost 50 countries, and another 300 were taken hostage. The ICRC has lost some 50 staff. One study of the impact of firearms on aid workers notes that "between July 2003 and July 2004 at least 100 civilian UN and NGO personnel died due to targeted violence."[65]

Afghanistan and Iraq are in a category by themselves regarding civilian personnel fatalities. In Afghanistan, at least 26 aid-agency staff died in 2004 alone.[66] The intrepid MSF decided that enough was enough and withdrew after five of its staff were murdered there in mid-2004. More recently, three insurgents dressed as police scaled a fence at the UN guesthouse in northern Afghanistan and killed five UN staff in a two-hour gun battle. And the eve of this book's going to press in August 2010 witnessed the grisly execution of 10 medical personnel working in the eastern province of Badakshan for the International Assistance Mission. In the Introduction we referred to the two cowardly assaults in Iraq in 2003 that shook humanitarians to the core: the 19 August 2003 attack on UN headquarters in Baghdad that resulted in 22 fatalities, including the charismatic head of the mission, Sergio Vieira de Mello; and six weeks later, a car bomb delivered in a white ambulance painted with a red crescent symbol killed 15 at the ICRC's country headquarters.

And the list goes on. In August 2006, for example, 17 staff from Action Against Hunger were brutally murdered in Sri Lanka; their deaths were especially shocking because of their involvement in post-tsunami relief and not the civil war between the Sri Lankan armed forces and the Tamil Tigers. Another brazen attack shook the aid establishment in October 2009: five WFP staff died after a suicide attack in the program's offices in Islamabad.

Following the deaths of 17 UN staff in an attack on UN headquarters in Algiers in 2007, the former Algerian foreign minister and veteran UN handyman Lakhdar Brahimi was asked to chair the Independent Panel on Safety and Security of United Nations Personnel and Premises. The report's clear message was: the UN blue flag clearly no longer provides any safety—in fact, it seems to have become a target.[67]

When Jan Egeland arrived for his briefings before assuming his post as UN under-secretary-general for humanitarian affairs, which was the very day that the Baghdad headquarters was destroyed, he noted, "The age of innocence has gone...I had expected to spend all my energies in the UN on the security and survival of disaster and conflict victims, not the security and survival of our own UN staff."[68]

These trends and individual episodes have fueled a debate about whether the vulnerability of aid workers has increased in recent years. The beginning of an evidence-based response came in the form of the first thorough quantitative analysis of the past decade's trends. It confirmed that the number of attacks and fatalities had doubled between 1997 and 2005, but that such an increase had to reflect the presence of more aid workers than ever before. Specifically, "the annual number of victims per 10,000 aid workers in the field averaged five in the first half of the period and six in the second."[69] There is also some evidence that NGOs were more likely to be targeted, but with considerable variation, and the cases of Afghanistan and Iraq are outliers distorting the average.

It is even more difficult to measure the costs of contemporary conditions on the psychological health of aid workers. Most relief agencies are adding mental health treatment, especially for post-traumatic stress disorder. This reality as well as a reported increase in suicide rates among humanitarian personnel is disquieting to say the least. Such information falls, of course, into the domain of privacy for staff members and their families, and so no real data are available. However, anecdotal evidence (in conversations with practitioners) suggests that some of the same types of pressures that have led to substantial psychological disorders and record suicide rates among the US military as a result of the occupation of Iraq and Afghanistan may also characterize the situation of aid workers.

In the most recent update of these statistics in 2009, Abby Stoddard, Adele Harmer, and Victoria DiDomenico found that attacks had increased sharply over 2006–2008—almost a doubling in deaths and kidnapping from the previous three years—with rates being especially bad for NGO expatriate staff and UN local contractors. Three conflicts (Darfur, Afghanistan, and Somalia) accounted for some 60 percent of the violence and victims.[70]

What has caused this increase? The reasons for today's danger are various. Some humanitarians point to "new" wars, other aid workers to the too close association with states and militaries, and still others to banditry and personal grudges. In many war-torn societies with Muslim majorities, such as Afghanistan and Iraq, the UN has come to be perceived as serving the interests of the major powers and applying a double standard by using force against them while doing virtually nothing to enforce long-standing resolutions in favor of Palestinians against Israel. What definitely seems new is the "performance" value of violent attacks on humanitarians.[71]

Much outrage in the West tends to focus on expatriate aid workers when, in fact, a growing percentage of agency personnel are increasingly drawn from vulnerable local populations. Indeed, to the extent that Western aid workers remove or distance themselves from the field, the distribution of risk might be shifting toward locally recruited workers. In any case, aid personnel can no longer assume (if they ever could) that their good intentions give them immunity.[72]

Conclusion: embarking on an unfinished journey

This chapter presents a range of struggles over definitions and identities as well as the contests about who qualifies as "humanitarian." A discussion of the quantitative and qualitative growth that has characterized the humanitarian industry over the past two decades followed a discussion of our three chronological periods that coincide with its birth and maturation, evolution, and turbulent years following the end of the Cold War. Finally, we spelled out the forces of destruction, production, and salvation as our preferred analytical lenses, the predominant factors circumscribing the efforts to save strangers.

With this basic knowledge in the reader's analytical toolkit, we are ready to embark on an historical humanitarian journey, one that remains and will remain unfinished. The first leg begins early in the nineteenth century and is followed by the battle of Solferino and continues with the two world wars of the first half of the twentieth century.

2 "Birth" and maturation, 1864–1945

- **Background**
- **The battle of Solferino**
- **Humanitarian intervention in the age of colonialism**
- **World War I: adolescence**
- **World War II: maturity**
- **Conclusion: toward a new era?**

In many respects it makes no more sense to speak of the birth of humanitarianism than, say, the birth of capitalism, nationalism, liberalism, sovereignty, or any other sort of longstanding set of beliefs that have been institutionalized in everyday life. For many, however, modern humanitarianism begins with the creation of the International Committee of the Red Cross in 1864. From where did the idea for the ICRC come?

Henry Dunant deserves considerable credit, but exactly how much is a matter of dispute. He certainly did not act on his own; he received considerable help from his friends, other Swiss intellectuals and businessmen. He also happened to have the right message at the right time. What background conditions created the opportunity?

Undoubtedly various changes in the nature of war, technology, and national societies played a key role in the emergence of the ICRC as a solution to a set of problems facing states and their societies. In addition, Dunant was tapping into a burgeoning ethic of care to distant strangers, evident not only in the growing sympathy for fallen soldiers but also in the movement to abolish the slave trade, which reached its climactic peak in the 1830s.

This chapter provides an overview of the creation and subsequent evolution of humanitarianism through the two world wars of the twentieth century. Our story is influenced by two choices. The first is that while many associate the beginning of humanitarianism with Dunant, we draw the reader's attention to developments over the preceding half-century because they highlight changes that created a favorable climate for the ICRC and the beginnings of a tradition of humanitarianism that aspired to do more than save soldiers. Second, we are interested in the great trends and historical shifts that made possible the changes in the character of humanitarianism.

In doing so we do not want to minimize the achievements of those moral visionaries who refused to take "impossible" for an answer. However, we do want to emphasize, following Karl Marx's famous aphorism, how these visionaries made history but not necessarily under conditions of their own choosing. We highlight the sweeping and imposing historical forces that combined to make humanitarianism imaginable, conceivable, and practical. Contemporary humanitarian action was born from the confluence of forces of production, destruction, and salvation (alongside medical advances and the growing ability to save strangers), factors that we stress throughout the book.

Background

Although expressions of charity, philanthropy, and care are as old as human history, beginning in the late eighteenth century European society underwent a series of disorienting changes that created the conditions for the emergence of modern humanitarianism. Although every age seems to worry that its social fabric is unraveling, rapid industrialization, urbanization, and modernization threatened traditional society, seemingly replacing religious mores and sensibilities with all kinds of social ills, including drunkenness, cruelty to animals and people, prostitution, and public brawling. At a time when "secularism" was still in its infancy, many of those who were most worried were religious leaders and those who were deeply influenced by the changing religious ideas of the time. Particularly important was the emergence of evangelicalism, a branch of Protestantism which, among other things, argued that it was necessary for humans to save themselves, spread the message, and use good works to foster heaven on earth. In addition, various intellectuals, politicians, jurists, and clergy began to adopt the discourse of humanity to describe their preferred social and political reforms as well as to push for public interventions to alleviate suffering and restore society's moral fiber.

Changes in the organization of society, the economy, and culture created new problems, and various elites and social movements responded with proposals for new solutions. Prior to the nineteenth century, most alms were given by religious authorities to the poor to help them stave off starvation, disease, and exposure. Beginning in the nineteenth century, however, charity became more public and organized and directed at removing the causes of suffering—in other words, charity became part of social reform. Social movements of all kinds emerged, including those concerned with temperance, charity for the poor, child labor regulations, urban reform, sanitation and hygiene, and mass education.[1] Although some had relatively modest ambitions, many aimed to save individuals, societies, and Christianity.

Importantly, many of the same reform societies, social movements, and leaders who spearheaded campaigns to humanize domestic society also became deeply troubled by unnecessary suffering outside their borders. The abolitionist movement was the most celebrated of all. This is not the place to describe the movement in depth, but three elements deserve mention because they portend future trends. First, during this time many in the anti-slavery movement called themselves "humanitarians," which broadly signified their desire to relieve unnecessary suffering. Consequently, the meaning of "humanitarianism" was more expansive than the one that would come to be associated with the ICRC.

Second, abolitionists were doing something quite remarkable for their times, campaigning to end the suffering of people whom they had never met and who belonged to different races, religions, and cultures. There is a range of explanations for why they did so—including changing religious beliefs, a desire to restore Britain's prestige after the loss of its American colonies, and domestic groups' ulterior political and economic purposes. It is important, nevertheless, to recognize how radical such thinking was for the times. There also is a range of explanations for why and how they were successful at persuading the British public. Some argued that it was a costless gesture because slavery was increasingly inefficient and unprofitable, while others contended that the British public was genuine in demonstrating new forms of empathy.

Third, many abolitionists were not content just to free the slaves but also wanted to improve their welfare. After all, what good was freedom if recently liberated men and women remained "uncivilized"? After years of diligent efforts and many setbacks, the abolitionists won a major victory in 1833. They were not so naïve to believe that the passage of the Abolition of Slavery Act would end bondage as they knew it; and they continued to fight against other forms of exploitation that amounted to slave-like conditions. Many abolitionists were also fervent missionaries outside of their home countries.

Missionaries are frequently stereotyped as sanctimonious servants of God who are blind to their own ideology and imperialists because they believed that "advanced" Christian peoples had a duty and responsibility

to save "backward" populations. The picture, however, is more complicated. Along with their efforts to carry their religious message forward
to non-Western peoples, they also introduced schools and public health
clinics; championed commerce; and imagined a moment when local
populations could be self-governing. In fact by the end of the nineteenth century, some missionary movements de-emphasized conversion
and concentrated on improving the lives of local populations.[2] Moreover, while missionaries could benefit from working with colonial
administrators and foreign merchants, they also were aware that such
"civilized" members of society could be downright uncivilized and
un-Christian toward local citizens. Some missionaries were outraged by
the un-Christian behavior of foreign merchants who engaged in debauchery
and exploitation.[3]

Indeed, colonial administrators and merchants often tried to limit
the activities of missionaries precisely because they could potentially
foment political unrest.[4] A handful of missionaries, for example, bravely
and single-handedly started a largely unsuccessful campaign against
King Leopold to stop the genocide in the Belgian Congo. And there
were instances in which missionaries called for colonial intervention
that state leaders believed was against their imperial interests. For
example, the British population desired to stamp out the slave trade,
which led to the ill-fated expedition to the Sudan in 1882, an expedition
opposed by British prime minister William Gladstone.[5] In this regard,
the missionaries of the colonial period foreshadowed contemporary
humanitarians.

The battle of Solferino

If war-related international humanitarianism had an inaugural moment,
it was in the aftermath of a bloody battle in northern Italy in 1859. In
response to the appalling scenes of fallen and maimed soldiers on the
Italian battlefield of Solferino, humanitarian activists pursued an
immediate goal—to convince states to give them access to populations at
risk. The popularity and resonance of the idea were immediate; within
a few years the grassroots campaign produced the ICRC and the Geneva
Conventions.

What Swiss businessman Henry Dunant would call in his 1862 self-
published book *Un souvenir de Solferino* (a memory of Solferino) led
the following year to the founding of the International Committee for
Relief to the World. Shortly thereafter, in 1864 the Swiss government
convened a diplomatic conference to expand "international" coverage
of the effort and thus invited all European countries as well as the

United States, Mexico, and Brazil, which resulted in a change in the organization's name to the International Committee of the Red Cross, the very first Geneva Convention to circumscribe the conduct of war, and the foundations of international humanitarian law.[6]

From then on officials and intellectuals hoped to expand the laws of war into new areas. One way to protect soldiers was to limit the kinds of weapons that could be used. Such initiatives, though, proved unpopular. An unsuccessful effort at a diplomatic gathering in Brussels in 1874 to consider a draft to further limit the decision to go to war and its conduct, drawn up by Russian czar Alexander II, met with more success later. The draft formed the basis for the 1899 and 1907 Hague Conventions, providing additional momentum to the growing body of international customary law as well as legal conventions constraining the conduct of war. Although delegates failed to reach any general agreement on arms limitations, they adopted a number of specific measures, including a prohibition against launching projectiles and explosives from the air, the use of projectiles to diffuse asphyxiating gases, and expanding bullets. These efforts, however, did not directly address the possibility of going to war to foster supposedly more humanitarian outcomes.

Humanitarian intervention in the age of colonialism

There certainly is no shortage of illustrations in which humanitarian justifications were used by foreign political and economic interests. One of the most famous—if only because of the sheer scale of the horror—occurred in the Congo Free State, a private project that benefited Belgium's King Leopold II. At the Berlin Conference of 1884–85, colonial powers agreed to turn the largest territory in Africa over to a European monarch with the expressed condition that the Congolese be brought into the modern world. Leopold abolished slavery but ran the Congo brutally for his own personal profit and aggrandizement. He amassed a personal fortune through ivory and rubber, and justified his genocidal exploitation involving the direct and indirect deaths of millions by advancing civilization as a humanitarian project.[7]

The entanglement of humanitarianism and the growing Great Power scramble for colonies gave birth to a term that would become quite familiar a century later, "humanitarian intervention." Specifically, many colonial powers rationalized the use of military force in humanitarian terms, but they often chose areas in which they had immediate strategic and economic interests and stayed long after the country was out of immediate danger.

References to humanitarian intervention first began to appear in the international legal literature in the mid-nineteenth century.[8] Two interventions in particular were most directly responsible for the emergence of this discourse: the intervention in Greece by England, France, and Russia in 1827 to stop Turkish massacres and suppression of populations associated with insurgents; and the intervention by France in Syria in 1860 to protect Maronite Christians.[9] In fact, there were at least five prominent interventions undertaken by European powers against the Ottoman Empire from 1827 to 1908.[10] By the 1920s, the rationale for intervention had broadened to include the protection of nationals abroad.[11]

An accepted theme that emerged from these early interventions was that intervention could be justified when a state abused its sovereignty by brutally and cruelly treating either nationals or foreigners within its territorial jurisdiction. Such a state was regarded as having made itself liable to action by any state or states that were prepared to intervene. One writer in 1921 depicted humanitarian intervention as "the reliance upon force for the justifiable purpose of protecting the inhabitants of another state from the treatment which is so arbitrary and persistently abusive as to exceed the limits of that authority within which the sovereign is presumed to act with reason and justice."[12]

Such intervention was surrounded by controversy, and many continue to look askance at the earliest cases of so-called humanitarian intervention.[13] Critics argued that humanitarian justifications were usually a pretext for pursuing strategic, economic, or political interests. Furthermore, there can be no doubt that even when more justifiable humanitarian objectives were present, the paternalism of intervening powers—self-appointed custodians of morality and human conscience as well as the guarantors of international order and security—undermined the credibility of the enterprise. This legacy continues to color the debate for, as Ramesh Thakur points out, developing countries "are neither amused nor mindful at being lectured on universal human values by those who failed to practice the same during European colonialism and now urge them to cooperate in promoting 'global' human rights norms."[14]

Because interests are closely associated with the decision by a state to intervene on humanitarian grounds, some insist that humanitarian interventions are always driven by power not principle. One noted legal authority concluded in 1963 that "no genuine case of humanitarian intervention has occurred with the possible exception of the occupation of Syria in 1860 and 1861."[15] The scale of the atrocities in that case may well have warranted intervention—more than 11,000 Maronite

Christians were killed and 100,000 made homeless in a single four-week period. By the time the 12,000 European soldiers had deployed, however, the violence was largely over; and after undertaking some relief activities, the troops withdrew.

Some legal commentators have held that a doctrine of humanitarian intervention existed in customary international law by the end of the nineteenth century, but a considerable number of scholars have disagreed. Some have argued that the doctrine was clearly established in state practice prior to 1945 and that only the parameters, not the existence, of the doctrine are open to debate. Others have rejected this claim, noting both the inconsistency in state practice, particularly in the twentieth century, and the substantial number of legal scholars who outright rejected the proposition. Clearly the notion of intervention developed substantially before the appearance of an international system with institutions responsible for maintaining international order and protecting human rights. Despite its continued conceptual and rhetorical evolution, national interests remain at its core in practice.

World War I: adolescence

Prior to World War I, most of the attempted innovations in emergency relief concerned civilizing war by outlawing and regulating certain kinds of military technologies and improving the conditions of wounded and captured soldiers. We have already seen the significant step forward with *jus in bello* (the laws of war) that began with the 1864 signing of the first Geneva Convention and its further advancement with the Hague Conventions of 1899 and 1907. Not only did these initiatives largely fail to protect soldiers, as would be clear beginning in 1914, but they did not cover the protection of civilians; it would not be until after World War II that states felt the need to extend protections to civilians during war.

In several respects, World War I was something of a way station between humanitarianism's past and future. There were three trends. To begin, states and relief agencies were only beginning to recognize what are now viewed as the sacrosanct principles of humanitarianism—impartiality, neutrality, and independence. Certainly the ICRC had been gravitating toward them, even if they were fairly inchoate, and it would be another half-century before they obtained any real precision. For the most part, during and after the war, governments tended to favor those institutions that lined up with their strategic interests, and societies mobilized on behalf of populations with whom they already had an established bond. British and American-based relief organizations, for example, focused exclusively on the needs of populations opposed to Germany and its allies. The US government-established quasi-private relief agency, the American Relief Administration (ARA), also intentionally neglected the needs of the civilian population in Germany; it was largely up to German-American associations to do that job.

Two initiatives in particular distinguished themselves because they insisted on the principles of impartiality, neutrality, and independence—albeit not for entirely identical reasons. Herbert Hoover, the American businessman and future president, worked heroically to mobilize aid on behalf of civilian populations facing famine in German-occupied Belgium and northern France. Because of the occupation and the slow-down of the economy, disruption of food production, a flood, and a blockade of the North Sea ports imposed by the Allies, Belgium was inflicted by a massive famine. Local relief organizations attempted to do what they could, but they were overwhelmed by the task of keeping alive over 9 million people. Living in London at the time, in September 1914, Hoover agreed to help secure a shipment of grain. This one modest gesture soon turned into the largest relief operation that the world had witnessed until that time—the Commission for Relief in Belgium (CRB). In order to get food into occupied Belgium, Hoover had to convince the British that relief would go to the civilian population and not the German military; at the same time, he had to persuade the Germans that food aid would not advantage the Allies. Toward that end, he got the combatants to recognize the CRB's political neutrality and operational independence.[16]

The other notable event was the founding of Save the Children by the British social reformer Eglantyne Jebb. In contrast to the long-time trend among the British to provide relief to its allies, Jebb insisted that children were innocent, humanity's future, and deserving of support regardless of their nationality. Eventually her views would no longer be treated as eccentric but rather commonplace.

A second trend was the growing role of states in the delivery and regulation of relief. Although prior to the war states had not neglected humanitarian action, they were hardly interested; the war would open their eyes to the potential and importance of aid. States began to fund relief in unprecedented amounts. Their newfound interest in relief was due not to any change of heart but rather to a growing awareness that they could harness the humanitarian spirit for their broader foreign policy goals. The logic was not altered after the war, when Hoover headed the ARA, which initially helped respond to the famine in Europe and Russia.[17] Like previous and future efforts, it appended charity with political ambitions and economic interests. Hoover and others saw relief as a way to gain influence in Russia and possibly undermine the Bolsheviks, while US Congressmen and farmers were hoping to find markets for American agriculture.[18]

In addition to and because of these pull factors, a third trend was the increased interest of states to develop multilateral organizations and laws that represented a combination of interests and norms. There was growing international sympathy for the plight of many populations who had not only suffered during wartime but who now had no home to return to. Accordingly, domestic societies were lobbying their governments to show a little tenderness. In addition, because of the assumption that humanitarian emergencies were probably here to stay in one form or another, states began to expect that they would be asked to do more and more.

Multilateral solutions had several advantages. They could give the appearance that states were doing something, but also ensure that states did no more than they wanted to do. In other words, they could help put limits on generosity. International organizations could help share the burden and thus make sure that no single state ended up carrying the load. They could help states make it appear that they wanted to act while organizations could cover up indifference—that is, multilateral organizations could become forums for making it seem as if states cared and legitimate decisions to do little or nothing.

These forces help to account for what is arguably the most important postwar innovation, the High Commission for Refugees (HCR). Growing state controls over their borders, a world war that created unprecedented numbers of displaced, the breakdown of the multinational empires (in Russia, Austria-Hungary, and Turkey), the creation of national states (often by ethnic cleansing), the Russian Revolution, and widespread famine created a specter in which millions of people were unable to either go home or find sanctuary. In 1921 the League of Nations responded by establishing the HCR. States decided to act for two principal reasons. Overwhelmed by the sheer number of displaced persons and their demands, many private charities lobbied states to create a new international agency.[19] Perhaps most important, states believed that mass population movements threatened to destabilize Europe. Yet there were limits on who would be helped. Although refugees were strewn across Europe, Western states were unwilling to recognize their presence and restricted HCR's mandate to Russian refugees. Also, the category of "refugee" was defined in part as someone forced to flee because of persecution—a politically loaded charge that participating governments were prepared to level only at Moscow. States also limited the HCR to coordination and refused to give it any operational capacity. Because HCR was not expected to do all that much, the budget was meager.

Despite its shackles, the HCR managed to break away somewhat and expand its scope. It ventured far beyond the Russian crisis and articulated a set of refugee rights. The organization's first high commissioner, the renowned Norwegian explorer Fridtjof Nansen, deserves much of the credit. In part because of his previous experience dealing with the repatriation of Russian war prisoners, he had credibility with Western governments that he exploited to expand the agency's activities. Over the objections of governments, Nansen soon insinuated himself into the political and refugee crises in Greece, Turkey, Bulgaria, and elsewhere. His actions proved to be a powerful precedent for international involvement in refugee issues. In addition to this geographical expansion, the HCR successfully negotiated a set of refugee rights, including travel documents (the so-called Nansen passport), education, and employment (Nansen worked with the International Labour Organization to help refugees find jobs).

For the first time, there thus was an international agency that was assisting refugees—helping to define populations in need and their rights. However, while the HCR was able to broaden its geographic scope, elevate issues, and set agendas, it remained a coordinating agency without any implementation capacity. It was wholly dependent on states to carry out its recommendations. When states refused to cooperate, little happened—the HCR's inability to assist those fleeing Nazi Germany demonstrated this reality with heartbreaking poignancy.

In general, among the trends in humanitarianism unleashed by World War I, perhaps none was more important than the establishment of new principles and the increased role of states in humanitarian action. From one angle these twin developments appear to be running at cross-purposes. If states are becoming more important to humanitarianism, then are not the principles of impartiality, independence, and neutrality undermined? From another angle, though, it is precisely because of the growing role of states that these principles have assumed more salience. If humanitarianism is to accomplish its immediate goal of gaining access to populations in need—especially given increased state involvement in humanitarian action, then it is absolutely vital that relief organizations find what would later be called "humanitarian space." World War I was a sign of the times as well as a harbinger of an ever-expanding industry.

World War II: maturity

World War II proved to be a moment when the very specter of rampant inhumanity led the so-called international community of sovereign states, propelled by civil society clamoring for a more stable planet, to imagine and aspire to a different future. The resulting surge in institution-building should not, of course, be viewed as an unadulterated triumph of humanitarianism. After all, the demand for new institutions, international laws, and inspirational calls-to-arms reflected the utter desecration of the idea of humanity after having turned Enlightenment principles on their head—what could be more of a caricature than science seeking the most efficient technology to exterminate peoples or experiments to create a master race? That said, death marches, concentration camps, the Holocaust, the fire bombings, and finally the use of nuclear weapons led not only activists but also diplomats to call for the protection of civilians and the dispossessed, for the restoration of basic human dignity.

The construction of the rule of law on the embers of World War II was not intended as a house of cards but rather a solid foundation for a better and more humane world order. The renewal of human values paved the way for such normative humanitarian pillars as the 1945 UN Charter and, almost immediately following the UN's birth, the 1948 Universal Declaration of Human Rights, the 1948 Convention on the Prevention and Punishment of the Crime of Genocide, and the 1949 Geneva Conventions (and eventually the 1977 Additional Protocols).[20]

We should also recall the humanitarian implications of the first restrictions on recourse to war, somewhat prematurely in the 1928 Kellogg-Briand Pact. Later the system crystallized into its current form under the United Nations Charter. Since 1945, the threat or use of force against the territorial integrity and political independence of states has been prohibited by Charter Article 2 (4), with exceptions granted for the collective use of force under Chapter VII and individual or collective self-defense in the event of an armed attack by Article 51. Although the prohibition seems clear, questions about the legality of humanitarian intervention remained. In 1946, for example, the eminent legal scholar Hersch Lauterpacht continued to argue that intervention was legally permissible when a state was guilty of cruelties against its nationals that denied their fundamental human rights and shocked the conscience of humankind.[21]

There also was an impressive growth in intergovernmental and non-governmental humanitarian machinery. The UN Relief and Rehabilitation Administration (UNRRA) was developed in 1943 from the remnants of the League's efforts to provide assistance to refugees in Europe who did not plan to be repatriated to the countries from which they had been displaced. The Food and Agriculture Organization, founded in 1943, was conceived to share information on agriculture and related technology as part of a larger global plan to prevent famines from triggering strife. And in 1942 a group of Quakers founded the Oxford Committee for Famine Relief (later shortened to Oxfam) to respond to the Greek famine.

The importance of the traditional principles espoused by the ICRC played a role far beyond the Red Cross (and eventually Red Crescent) Movement because its principles and persona became synonymous with "humanitarianism." Indeed, while the meaning differs from dictionary to dictionary, in 1986 the International Court of Justice, for a case brought by Nicaragua against the United States, decided that it would be better not to come up with a legal definition for the term; the world court simply referred to the ICRC's principles and work as synonymous with humanitarianism.[22]

Conclusion: toward a new era?

In the postwar period, the groundwork was prepared for a period of stability and prosperity with the rule of law through a second generation of international organizations of the United Nations system, including humanitarian ones. The initial hopes for world peace with a more humanitarian face, however, were soon dashed as the Iron Curtain fell across Europe. The Cold War ensued, and displaced and suffering peoples were hardly a thing of the past. And as Washington and Moscow confronted each other through proxies, ever new humanitarian crises emerged in flashpoints around the globe.

3　The traditional enterprise, 1945–89

- **Background**
- **Humanitarian action during the Cold War: selected cases**
- **Tensions within the humanitarian enterprise and with states**
- **Conclusion: the end of the "golden years"**

As we just saw, World War II caused the international community of states to long for a better future, but their visions were hardly utopian. Skeptics often view multilateral cooperation as frivolous in comparison with the red meat of world politics, namely national interests and *Realpolitik*. Politicians and people as well as pundits have forgotten that the actual birth of the "United Nations" was not the signing of the UN Charter on 26 June 1945 in San Francisco, but rather the adoption of the "Declaration by the United Nations" in Washington, DC, on 1 January 1942. There and then, the same 26 countries of the powerful coalition that would defeat fascism anticipated the formal establishment of a world organization as an essential extension of their wartime commitments. After the failure of the League of Nations and the Great Depression, states did not view the construction of international order in the form of the UN system as a liberal plaything to be tossed aside when the going got rough but rather a vital necessity for postwar order and prosperity. Humanitarianism was an integral part of that vision. We want to stress, however, how inimical state interests were (and remain).

The presentation of our second historical period, 1945–89, begins with an overview as a prelude to illustrating through several key case studies the types of tensions that arose within the international humanitarian system and between it and the system of states. Today many humanitarians look back upon those 45 years as some type of "golden age." Their nostalgia resembles that of some analysts of international peace and security who also long for the warm blanket and predictability of the Cold War. But we are getting ahead of our story.

Background

As we saw, the humanitarian crises that accompanied World War II continued to spur the development of the humanitarian system. The UN Charter's Preamble aspired "to save succeeding generations from the scourge of war, which twice in our lifetime has brought untold sorrow." The sadly hollow character of that soaring prose meant that the late 1940s and beyond hardly spelled the end of the need for humanitarian action—quite the contrary.

In the early postwar years, a host of new intergovernmental organizations (IGOs) joined the United Nations family; and even more significant numerically was the spike in growth and influence of NGOs. At the same time, states created new international legal instruments (e.g., the 1948 UN Convention on the Prevention and Punishment of the Crime of Genocide) and fashioned iterations of international humanitarian law to reflect the realities of recent conflicts. The updates of the Geneva Conventions in 1949, and again with the Additional Protocols in 1977, elaborated earlier rights and protections and ultimately enlarged those covered to include civilians and civil wars.

A central and potentially liberating idea present at the creation of the United Nations ultimately resulted in much new business for the humanitarian enterprise: that peoples in all countries had the inherent right to be politically independent. The end of colonization and the achievement of sovereignty came within the UN's first two decades and for almost all other countries by 1980. Instead of the 51 original signatories of the Charter in 1945, there are flags from 192 countries currently flying in front of UN headquarters. The initial euphoria of independence has subsequently been replaced by the difficulties of fragile and failed states and civil wars; but that tragic humanitarian blow-back is more central to the story in the next chapter.

Decolonization and the emergence of development discourse also fed into a desire to reduce suffering in what was not yet called the "Third World" or "global South."[1] Development became, to some, a novel tool to combat the twin scourges of war and inequality, the new just cause. This emphasis was especially noteworthy as the heating up of the Cold War made virtually impossible not only collective security through the United Nations—the theory of an all-against-one and automatic use of international force against an aggressor—but also impeded collaboration on international peace and security other than the occasional use of peacekeepers when warring parties consented to their acting as buffers or monitors of agreements.

Instead, development became the UN's primary business.[2] The World Bank—whose initials remain IBRD, International Bank for Reconstruction and Development—was founded to "reconstruct" and "develop" Europe but soon expanded enormously the geographic and substantive reach of its development activities to newly independent countries that had not been the scenes of battle but had different challenges. As mentioned earlier, many relief organizations established in response to the needs of the victims of Europe's wars became engrossed in promoting economic and social development in the Third World. Oxfam, CARE, and CRS all got their start providing relief during World War II and then turned their attention to poverty alleviation and development. Cynics would lament "mission creep" by opportunistic agencies, but the pressing needs on the ground led to a demand-driven adaptation by institutions that already had a strong track record.

Although we are primarily interested in organizations that have a direct bearing on humanitarian action, it is necessary to place the creation of relevant agencies and public international law within the broader political context of that time. The establishment of the UN family was the most visible and significant indicator of a seismic political-historical moment. Based on the admittedly overly idealistic organizing principle of collective security, it underlined the potential of the norms and practices of robust international cooperation that had worked well among wartime allies. This normative and institutional framework allowed several crucial components of the international humanitarian system to be nested within universal-membership organizations with a global presence and for NGOs to work in complementary and supplementary ways.

As mentioned, in 1943 UNRRA grew from the remnants of the League's efforts to provide assistance to refugees in Europe who did not plan to be repatriated to the countries from which they had fled. It was revamped as the International Refugee Organization in 1947, which in turn underwent another makeover into the office of the UN High Commissioner for Refugees in 1951. At that time, its mandate was still temporary and its funding voluntary in order to mitigate the plight of the remaining postwar refugees in Europe. After the massive exodus of Hungarian refugees in 1956, it became obvious that displaced peoples were a permanent not temporary feature of the international system even in Europe—in fact, the UNHCR already had informally helped refugees from Algeria in Tunisia and from China in Hong Kong. The 1967 Protocol Relating to the Status of Refugees officially removed the temporal and geographical limits for the UNHCR; this marked the beginning of a truly multilateral refugee regime to protect refugees in the context of decolonization and Cold War proxy wars.[3]

The United Nations Children's Emergency Fund had a similar journey. States established it in 1946 to provide temporary assistance with voluntary funding to children in countries devastated by the war. However, the UN Children's Fund became a permanent fixture of the United Nations system in 1953, keeping its popular former acronym, UNICEF, in spite of the shortened name.

Private agencies also blossomed during the war and shortly thereafter. Quakers founded the Oxford Committee for Famine Relief (later Oxfam) in 1942 to respond to the wartime Greek famine, and it continued to expand its operations and country chapters. In 1945 what was first known as the Cooperative for American Remittances to Europe (CARE) was founded to send food relief to Europe to combat starvation. It then became the Cooperative for Assistance and Relief Everywhere, and finally simply CARE. It is currently one of the largest international NGOs—indeed, the original "CARE package" distributed by the organization has become a generic term for any parcel sent for relief or comfort or even to supposedly starving undergraduates by their parents.[4] Following the cessation of hostilities, other new NGOs materialized: Lutheran World Relief; Church World Service, a branch of the National Council of Churches; Catholic Relief Services; and Caritas International, a Catholic charity based at the Vatican. To provide relief to orphans in the Korean War, Christian groups formed World Vision in 1950. In short, both secular humanistic and religious sentiments helped launch a baby boom of private institutions.

During the 1950s, 1960s, and 1970s, other additions focused especially on emergency needs. In 1961, the World Food Programme was created to hasten rapid, short-term food aid, and to coordinate assistance for and with the Food and Agriculture Organization. What began as an ad hoc institutional invention of the moment became a formal and free-standing agency that (along with the UNHCR and UNICEF) is now one of the three largest UN relief organizations. Beyond food aid, other emergency assistance also required more extensive coordination among far-flung and quite independent UN agencies. In 1971, member states founded the UN Disaster Relief Organization to manage a gamut of tasks—assessing needs, mustering responses, cementing cooperation, and teaching preparedness and prevention.

In addition to institutions, the historical juncture of the late 1940s also spawned a host of international principles, practices, and laws that nourished the humanitarian impulse and facilitated the delivery of assistance and the provision of protection to affected populations worldwide. The trials of defeated powers in Germany and Japan were especially noteworthy. Instead of the preoccupation with the ability of the state to protect citizens against attack from other states, Jews in Germany were subject to unspeakable depredations by their own state authorities

in the 1930s and 1940s. Nazi Germany's slaughter of minority populations—its ideological fervor and industrial power threatening to exterminate entire peoples and cultures—led Raphael Lemkin in 1943 to coin
the term *genocide*, a combination of the Greek word for family, tribe,
or race and the Latin one for killing.[5] States gave legal voice to the
desire to prohibit such acts as genocide with the 1948 Convention on
the Prevention and Punishment of the Crime of Genocide defines as

> any of the following acts committed with intent to destroy, in whole
> or in part, a national, ethnical, racial or religious group, as such:
> killing members of the group; causing serious bodily or mental harm
> to members of the group; deliberately inflicting on the group con-
> ditions of life, calculated to bring about its physical destruction in
> whole or in part; imposing measures intended to prevent births within
> the group; [and] forcibly transferring children of the group to another
> group.

States have an easier time giving voice to their outrage than putting
muscle behind their words. Each of us can easily recall crimes perpetrated
by public authorities and peoples against their own kith and kin or those
permitted by others unwilling or unable to intervene. The "never again"
moments since World War II's Holocaust include Cambodia in this
historical period as well as Rwanda and Srebrenica in the next. States
might be better at talking than acting, but now they have to explain
their indifference and sometimes are embarrassed by their hypocrisy to
take action. We return to this topic in the next chapter as well, but it is
important to recall the historical moment that produced the term and
initial steps toward making "never again" more than a slogan.

The murder of Jews along with the sick, communists, Gypsies, and
homosexuals led to a postwar institutionalization of values that are in
two ways relevant for understanding humanitarian action, then and
now. Punishment and deterrence (or negative actions after the fact in
the hope of preventing future acts) in the form of the Tokyo and Nur-
emberg trials restricted the ability of states to hide behind sovereignty
as a cover for mass atrocity crimes and the systematic violation of human
rights. The brutality of World War II and Lemkin's work clearly struck
a chord within international society. A specialized body of international
humanitarian law developed to define the characteristics of genocide
and the legal responsibilities to prevent it. The Genocide Convention
was formulated in 1947–48 and approved by states one day earlier than
the Universal Declaration of Human Rights in December 1948. The
Universal Declaration was, in Michael Ignatieff's words, "designed to

create fire walls against barbarism"[6] and was followed by a host of other international conventions that enshrined the notion of common humanity.[7]

The laws of war (also collectively and euphemistically called "international humanitarian law") were updated after the experience of World War II. Given the extent of war crimes committed by numerous state parties, the Swiss government and the ICRC organized another Geneva conference in 1949 to strengthen and expand humanitarian protections. On 12 August four conventions were agreed and after sufficient ratification became law on 21 October 1950: the Amelioration of the Condition of the Wounded and Sick in Armed Forces in the Field (first convention); Amelioration of the Condition of the Wounded, Sick and Shipwrecked Members of Armed Forces at Sea (second); Relative to the Treatment of Prisoners of War (third); and Relative to the Protection of Civilian Persons in Times of War (fourth).

Like their predecessors—including the 1864 Geneva Convention, the 1899 and 1907 Hague Conventions, and the 1925 Geneva Protocol[8]—the 1949 conventions are constructed on the foundations of earlier principles and agreements but adapted to the peculiar political sensibilities and preoccupations of the post-1945 era. The unspeakable treatment of combatants and the captured inspired states to clarify and develop rights and protections for soldiers and POWs (prisoners of war). Common Article 13 of the First and Second Geneva Conventions stress the applicability of these regulations exclusively to official armed forces and those affiliated or tied to them. These provisions cover those who can be and are as accountable as states—meaning they seek international sanction for their status as legal combatants. Accordingly they must have a command structure, display distinctive signs and emblems indicating that they are belligerents, carry their weapons openly, and commit themselves to respect international humanitarian law.

Moreover, the enormous civilian toll of World War II also placed the status of unarmed parties firmly on the international agenda and then translated them into the precise language of public international law. Although the First, Second, and Third Geneva Conventions comprise most of the substance of the 1949 renovations, the Fourth Geneva Convention may actually have more wide-ranging implications, as it is the first international agreement that specifically protects civilians in war. In order to reflect various developments in contemporary warfare, these treaties were updated with two Additional Protocols in 1977, one for international and one for non-international (or civil) wars. Overall, the widespread popularity of and routine adherence to the 1949 Geneva Conventions and the Additional Protocols suggests that they effectively embody the norms of post-World War II order; the less than perfect compliance with them, as always, suggests that physical reality is distinct from normative rhetoric.

Humanitarian action during the Cold War: selected cases

Every card-carrying member of the international relations establishment will inform any captive student that every historical case is sui generis. Here, however, we hope to use key cases of the Cold War to illustrate the essential types of tensions present during the second historical period. Subsequently, as readers see, too many of the lessons have been conveniently airbrushed from humanitarian history.

The 1956 Hungarian Revolution

The international response to the refugee crisis following the Soviet invasion of Hungary in 1956 was an important learning experience for aid agencies. It helped to shape the way that humanitarians dealt with issues of refugee protection and resettlement during the Cold War. Moreover, the first major crisis faced by the recently incorporated and permanent Office of the UN High Commissioner for Refugees also sparked an international legal debate that led to a broadened definition of "refugee" from that initially envisaged in the 1951 Convention Relating to the Status of Refugees. Hungary also was the first humanitarian crisis to be viewed extensively on television, albeit on film and delayed rather than in real time as has been the case since the 1980s.

After the death of Stalin in 1953, Moscow began to slightly relax its rigid stance toward its Eastern European satellites. In Hungary, this meant accepting the replacement of the unpopular government by a more moderate communist faction, headed by Imre Nagy. While this was reversed by hard-liners forcing their own return to power in July 1956, an increasing wave of Hungarian nationalism and resentment toward the new government's harsh repression led to an uprising in October. Western media and governments—foreshadowing what they would do in later years by suggesting that they might actually come to the aid of dissidents when that clearly was out of the question—may have fomented more vocal and visible public revolt than would otherwise have been the case. A synonym for the phrase "moral hazard" is "hanging Hungarians out to dry."

After sending troops to quell opposition, the Soviet Union subsequently agreed to reinstate a moderate government. However, Moscow was ill-prepared for Nagy's independent stance, and its subsequent decision to remove him provoked still more violent resistance. Hungarians counting on an active helping hand from the West were soon disappointed. After a brief lull and the withdrawal of Soviet troops, the uprising continued and thousands of Soviet soldiers and tanks returned to Hungarian cities in early November, including the capital, Budapest. Lasting from 23 October to 10 November, the fighting claimed the lives of several thousand Hungarians, and thousands more were executed.[9]

Some 200,000 people fled the country, the vast majority heading to Austria and about 20,000 to Yugoslavia, before later dispersing to about 40 countries worldwide. The largest numbers of refugees were resettled in the United States, Canada, the United Kingdom, Australia, and Germany; but significant numbers also went to various South American and a couple of African states. As refugees from Soviet occupation, they were accorded immediate asylum—with no questions asked because they were helpful symbols of heavy-handed Soviet repression in the ongoing propaganda battle of West versus East.

To organize the massive relief and resettlement effort, a committee was established in Austria consisting of the UNHCR, the Intergovernmental Committee for European Migration (ICEM), the League of Red Cross Societies (now known as the International Federation of Red Cross and Red Crescent Societies), the Austrian government, and various NGOs. The overall effort was coordinated by the UNHCR, which also dealt with refugee resettlement within Austria. The Red Cross was the primary aid organization, while ICEM was tasked with documenting refugees and organizing the international resettlement effort.

An initially problematic legal issue was that the Refugee Convention was created to deal with displacement caused by World War II, and so its definition of "refugee" was someone who crossed an international boundary before 1951. Another legal issue was that refugee status was supposed to be individually assessed. However, the Austrian government and international agencies decided to apply the provisions of the convention across-the-board to Hungarians, a judgment to which the member states of the UN General Assembly, which had signed the convention, soon agreed. The ICEM also decided to enable group evaluation to speed-up the resettlement process, which aided the swift response by humanitarian agencies, with about half the total number of refugees being resettled in the first few months.

As well as the international refugee protection and resettlement work, some humanitarian agencies were also allowed into Hungary by Soviet authorities, during and after the uprising, to deal with immediate needs and to aid in feeding the disrupted population during the winter. The ICRC responded to a call for help from the Hungarian Red Cross by airlifting medical and other relief supplies to Budapest during the early, less violent days of the uprising. A representative of the ICRC was also able to meet with leaders of the uprising in the town of Györ, visit their POWs, and convince them to adhere to the Geneva Conventions with respect to POW treatment. As the crisis worsened, international organizations, including the UN General Assembly, condemned the Soviet response. The neutral ICRC soon became the only international agency with access to Hungary permitted by Moscow.

Biafra–Nigeria War

The 1968–70 Biafra–Nigeria civil war was a seminal event for humanitarian agencies, shaping debates about their philosophy and operating procedures for decades.[10] Looking back, one of the most respected analysts of humanitarian action Philip Gourevitch summarizes:

> In fact, the humanitarianism that emerged from Britain—and its lawyerly twin, the human rights lobby—is probably the most enduring legacy of the ferment of 1968 in global politics. Here was a non-ideological ideology of engagement that allowed, a quarter of a century after Auschwitz, not to be a bystander, and, at the same time, not to be identified with power: to stand always with the victim, in solidarity with clean hands—healing hands.[11]

It also foreshadowed some of the complex emergencies of the post–Cold War period. The thorny issues included the debate within the humanitarian community over how aid could contribute toward prolonging conflict and thereby suffering; how aid could be used for political/military purposes; and the value of neutrality versus speaking out about atrocities committed by belligerents. These controversies led to the creation of some agencies that have subsequently become significant players in the humanitarian arena, such as Médecins Sans Frontières and Concern Worldwide.

Nigeria became an independent state upon British withdrawal in 1960. Prior to British colonial rule, however, its territory had never been under the control of a single authority. Nigeria consists primarily of three relatively ethnically homogeneous and culturally distinct regions, with Hausa and Fulani people in the north, Yoruba in the southwest, and Ibo in the southeast.

Tensions between the political and military leaders of these groups grew in the years following independence. Each major ethnic group feared that a rival would control the whole country in such a way as to privilege their own ethnicity and region. A coup by Ibo military commanders in

January 1966 was followed by a counter-coup of Hausa commanders a few months later. The southeastern Ibo region declared independence in July 1967, calling itself the state of Biafra. This decision sparked a civil war, pitting the primarily Hausa and Yoruba units of the Nigerian Army against the Ibos.

The civil war generated a humanitarian disaster as famine resulted from the Nigerian Army's attempt to starve Biafra into submission by sealing off the renegade Ibo state. Not only were massacres of civilians and other atrocities committed by government forces, another estimated 2 million people died from starvation due to the blockade. "Genocide" was not a loosely used term then, but an accurate and widespread depiction of some 25,000 persons from a single ethnic group dying each day. After images of starving children hit the Western press, the Biafra famine became the first to be real-time news. This led to a significant response and provision of aid by Red Cross societies, Joint Church Aid (a faith-based relief NGO), and others. However, the United Nations did not participate—at that time assisting rebels would have been interpreted as an affront to a recognized government. Nor did donor governments directly aid Biafrans (only through donations to private agencies). The Biafran crisis thus became the first international humanitarian relief effort led by NGOs.

After one of its planes was shot down, the ICRC stopped humanitarian deliveries in 1969, well before the end of the war and the famine. The Nigerian government suspected that military support was disguised as humanitarian assistance and insisted that flights be inspected prior to departure for the Biafran region and only leave during daylight. Meanwhile the Biafran authorities refused to allow daytime flights. Nevertheless, agencies did not end up with secure control over aid delivery. Toward the end of the war, only Joint Church Aid was able to continue airlifting significant humanitarian supplies to the shrinking Biafra-controlled area.

The biggest aerial relief effort since the 1948–49 Berlin airlift, however, was controversial among humanitarians because delivering such supplies may have prolonged the war and thereby Ibo suffering. "Moral hazard" is a term used in economics to describe the possible result that the provision of insurance against risk unintentionally encourages the insured to act irresponsibly, based on the expectation that any short-term loss will be compensated by the subsequent insurance payment. We encountered this danger in the previous section in relationship to the false hopes created for Hungarians by Western governments that loudly voiced their support but had no intention of confronting the Soviet Union. Similarly, many humanitarians argued that helping Biafra fomented separatists and thus caused part of the tragic outcome that it intended to prevent.[12]

In addition to a lack of agreement among aid agencies over the best way to reduce suffering, some of those working for the ICRC in the war zones disapproved of its long-standing policy of public discretion—of not criticizing the government for the blockade that led to the famine or for the massacre of civilians. One of the most prominent and articulate dissidents was a French doctor, Bernard Kouchner, who broke the ICRC pledge of secrecy. He wrote angrily in the daily *Le Monde* about what he had witnessed. With colleagues he founded MSF in 1971 as an agency that would not be bound by the rules of neutrality in war zones, priding itself on speaking out against abuse whenever it occurred and without regard to the source.[13] This disagreement over neutrality also involved Oxfam, which blamed the British government's support for a united Nigeria as the cause of the conflict.

In the final analysis, it appears likely that the humanitarian relief effort during the civil war helped to prolong the conflict, thereby costing many lives. As Gourevitch crisply notes, "Had it not been for the West's charity, the Nigerian civil war surely would have ended much sooner."[14] It was also a profoundly unsettling experience for many agencies, and its lessons shaped subsequent debates among the various constituencies of the international humanitarian system. The controversies—especially whether aid workers were pawns whose aid had unintended consequences doing more harm than good, and whether agencies should bring attention to misconduct by the warring parties—continue to divide humanitarians today. At the same time, Paul Harvey cautions: "The idea that abusive, corrupt, or authoritarian regimes responsible for creating or ignoring humanitarian crises would show more concern for their citizens in the absence of international aid agencies is a largely unproveable counter-factual."[15]

Ethiopia

The Ethiopian famine marks the beginning of the role for prominent celebrities in publicizing humanitarian crises, which remains prevalent today in the form of UNICEF goodwill ambassadors such as Angelina Jolie or Bono in support of the Millennium Development Goals.[16] It also stimulated debate over when aid agencies should withdraw from an operational role on the ground, and the role of governments in creating famine. The latter point highlights the issue of agencies turning a blind eye to famine-creating war strategies in return for access to people suffering from it.

The 1983–85 Ethiopian famine, or more accurately famines, primarily in the north and southeast of the country, resulted in perhaps 1 million deaths, with several million more people displaced and diminished by malnutrition.[17] The government originally pointed to drought as the cause, an explanation widely accepted internationally during the crisis. In fact in 1984, there also was drought in the south and east of the country. While subsequently blamed for triggering the crisis, the famines had in fact begun earlier, especially in the north, where food production was not as adversely affected as elsewhere.

The famines stemmed primarily from the government's counter-insurgency campaigns against rebel groups and secession movements, especially in the north, and related political and economic factors, including the inability of vulnerable populations to have access to the food that was being produced. In addition to high prices, access was worsened by the government's blocking food supplies to rebel-held areas and to areas under government control thought to be sympathetic to insurgents. Moreover, when international aid arrived, the government diverted and sold some of it, again to help its war effort. As in the case of Biafra, the issue arose as to whether humanitarian agencies should work with those who caused the disaster in the first place. By keeping silent and agreeing to constraints on their actions, aid agencies may have abetted the government's war strategy.

As world attention was brought to the Biafran famine by media coverage of starving children, the Ethiopian famines were first highlighted globally by a news broadcast from the British Broadcasting Corporation (BBC) by reporter Michael Buerk in October 1984. However, the Ethiopian crisis gained far more attention as it quickly became a *cause célèbre*. Most prominent was rock musician Bob Geldof, who wrote the Band Aid song "Do They Know It's Christmas?" with fellow musician Midge Ure. Released in November that year, it became a huge success in the United Kingdom and internationally. A US charity single, "We Are the World," was released in March 1985 and also became a worldwide hit. Most significant, however, was the Live Aid fund-raising rock concert organized by Geldof and Ure and held simultaneously in London and Philadelphia on 13 July 1985. This unprecedented attention to the crisis heralded a new era in humanitarian fund-raising, with a heightened role for celebrity promotion and endorsement.

Unlike Biafra, donor governments coordinated aid while NGOs were more peripheral to a massive response. International donors had at first been skeptical of the Ethiopian government's appeals for aid due to the evidence of diversion of already-donated food supplies away from rebel-held areas, where most of the famines were occurring. However, international media attention encouraged an initially uncritical response by governments and humanitarian agencies. Nevertheless, it became increasingly apparent that aid was not reaching most of those affected. In fact, most food was going to soldiers and militia. MSF was becoming increasingly uneasy with the role of aid in perpetuating the conflict and enabling the government's policies of ethnic cleansing, and by 1985 it could no longer deny what was obvious. After going public with its criticisms, MSF was expelled by the Ethiopian government.

Disagreements arose among humanitarians over the advisability and legitimacy of decisions to withdraw because of such abuses rather than staying the course and making the most of limited opportunities. The government's aid diversion strategy was compounded by forced resettlement and other policies that significantly worsened the crisis and hurt civilians. Three years later, in 1988, the ICRC withdrew because its work in relocation camps contributed to a direct policy of forcible relocation of sections of the population that might have otherwise supported the rebels. The ICRC's assistance could therefore be interpreted as violating neutrality by supporting the government's war strategy.

Most humanitarian operators, however, maintained an official policy of neutrality, which thereby required not publicly criticizing the government. Aid agencies were therefore able to operate on the ground during the war but arguably contributed to worsening the situation. The balance between remaining silent to facilitate access to some victims or highlighting abuses by combatants (whether government or insurgent) as well as the pluses and minuses of withdrawal, continue to be debated by aid workers.

Afghanistan

In the 1980s, the refugee situation in Pakistan, where several million Afghanis had fled to following the Soviet invasion, demonstrates numerous difficulties encountered by humanitarians in maintaining neutrality, resisting the interference of powerful states, and preventing refugee camps from harboring combatants. These challenges too remain acute in contemporary humanitarian disasters.

An April 1978 coup d'état brought the communist People's Democratic Party of Afghanistan to power, which was followed by a coup within the governing party in September 1979. In order to restore what the Soviet government considered to be a more pro-Russian leader in its extended backyard, the Soviet Union invaded in December. However, it soon became embroiled in a guerilla war against the *mujahideen*, a loose coalition of Sunni Islamic fighters, Shia insurgents, and various other armed groups whose campaign eventually forced the army to withdraw in 1989, following what Soviet general-secretary Mikhail Gorbachev called "a bleeding wound."[18] Moscow's unsuccessful occupation and restoration of a territorially effective pro-Soviet government was a key event in the Soviet Union's overstretch and eventual implosion.

Hundreds of thousands and perhaps millions of Afghanis died directly or indirectly from the decade-long occupation, and millions more fled the country. Around 3 million were housed in camps in Pakistan alone, with many more in Iran and other surrounding countries. This massive flight was not just an unfortunate byproduct of war but also the result of a Soviet bombing campaign of settlements and infrastructure that sought to deprive insurgents of local support.[19]

In addition to their primary purpose of housing noncombatants who had fled the fighting, the refugee camps in Pakistan also effectively provided a base for *mujahideen* to rest in relative safety and to recruit for their guerilla war across the border. Support for refugees and insurgents was generously forthcoming from the West, especially from Washington, as part of the ongoing Cold War battle with the East. The families of resistance fighters could also live in the camps free from Soviet reprisals. Not only was the Pakistani government aware of this dual function of the camps, but also the Inter-Services Intelligence Directorate (ISI) of the country's military funneled weapons and helped train the *mujahideen* in Pakistan throughout the 1980s. The ISI even established separate training camps and coordinated financing and weapons from the US and Saudi governments as well as other sources. The United States especially was keen on keeping its role in financing the resistance to the Soviets a secret, and so the ISI provided a convenient cover as well as a coordinating mechanism. Pakistani government cooperation was stimulated by a military aid package that amounted to several billion dollars.

Pakistani authorities controlled the administration of the camps, allowing only the UNHCR to coordinate aid activities within them. The UNHCR's attempts to gain more independence and to diminish the insurgent use of the camps were hampered by the fact that Pakistan was not a party to the 1951 Convention Relating to the Status of Refugees. In addition, the government financed about half the cost of maintaining the camps. It also introduced an Afghan political dimension to relief, as it started to tie aid distribution to adherence to one or another Afghan political party. Washington encouraged this divide-and-rule Pakistani policy as a way to bring greater legitimacy to the Afghan resistance leadership. Ironically, in retrospect, radical Islamic groups in Afghan politics became more prominent as well.

Despite awareness on the ground of the dual function of the camps, aid agencies largely ignored the adverse implications of the insurgents' presence for the safety of the refugees and for the effective supply of combatants. For example, at an international symposium on the Afghan refugee crisis in Oxford in 1987, the issue of aid manipulation was not even on the agenda. Some aid agencies actively sympathized with the resistance as a just cause.

US government funding for UNHCR relief in the camps ultimately gave Washington influence over the organization's policy. Similarly, US funding for a variety of NGOs—including CRS, IRC, and CARE—was part of its strategy of aiding the Afghan resistance and helping the Pakistani government. The United States was especially concerned that Pakistan might try to reach an accommodation with the Soviet-backed government in Kabul. In the end, Pakistan gained substantially from hosting the largest refugee population in the world. In addition to massive US military aid, the international community of states largely overlooked the government's poor human rights record as it earned more widespread legitimacy by providing relief to the victims of conflict and oppression.

Afghan resistance groups in Pakistan were encouraged to work together by the Saudi and US governments, for whom a show of unity was a concrete indication of the value of aid in the diplomatic battle against not only Moscow's occupation but Soviet ideology more generally. However, what little unity that was achieved did not outlive the Soviet withdrawal by much, with local commanders in Afghanistan soon fighting each other. Continued strife was widespread, essentially with no central government until the Islamist Taliban took control of most of Afghanistan in the late 1990s.

The Afghan refugee crisis highlights the complications arising from aid agencies' operating in a disaster zone where powerful states are involved, militarily and diplomatically, and are willing to employ aid directly to pursue their own interests and fund aid agencies willing to use such resources.[20] While there are rarely if ever pure motivations behind massive assistance, in this case the manipulation of humanitarians was so substantial that agencies clearly should have asked more questions and insisted on more autonomy. The dilemmas arising from the dual function of camps unfolded again in the Rwandan Hutu refugee camps in Zaïre in the mid-1990s.

Sudan

During the civil war in Sudan, the main international relief coordinating agency was the UN's Operation Lifeline Sudan (OLS), which successfully negotiated with both main warring factions for access to civilians. This heralded a new era of the UN's delivering aid on both sides of a conflict zone and in negotiating with nonstate armed groups.[21]

In 1983 civil war broke out between the Sudanese government and a southern rebel group, the Sudan People's Liberation Army (SPLA). The government was, and still is, largely controlled from the capital Khartoum by Arabic-speaking Muslim groups dominant in the north, while the SPLA, fighting to control the south, was started by mutinous army units representing mainly Christian and animist groups in that region. The second civil war in the country since independence from British rule in 1956 partly stemmed from the government's reduction of the autonomy that the south had been granted in the Addis Ababa Agreement, which had ended the previous war in 1972. The government also attempted to impose Sharia law, which was vehemently opposed by the largely non-Muslim south. This region also has more fertile land and, more recently discovered, substantial oil fields. Clearly, the central government in Khartoum was keen to maintain not only access to but control over such resources.

Eventually, and after more than 20 years of violent conflict, a peace agreement was signed in 2005, creating a coalition government including members of the SPLA's political wing, the Sudan People's Liberation Movement (SPLM). The agreement also included a referendum on independence in the south in 2011. The human cost of the civil war was staggering: approximately 2 million people died from armed conflict and famine, and over 4 million were displaced.[22] And peace remains tenuous.

We return here to the 1980s because the famine was partly a byproduct of the armed conflict, as farmers became unable to work their land. However, famine was also a weapon of war as it had been in Biafra and Ethiopia. Supplied with weapons by the government, Arab militia groups raided the south, killed indiscriminately, and destroyed cattle and other food sources while preventing the population from leaving to seek food elsewhere. Mass starvation resulted among survivors, with some areas almost completely depopulated. In some instances, government officials also denied refugees from the south access to relief supplies; and trains full of refugees were attacked by northern militias.

SPLA attacks also displaced large numbers of people. For example, in 1986 alone over 100,000 people fled to the north and a similar number to Ethiopia. Drought the following year in the south resulted in even more starvation and flight. After a coup in 1989 by elements of the military backed by a northern political party, the National Islamic Front, the famine in the north worsened and during the next year affected most of the country. Government food policy exacerbated the situation.

Media coverage in the West and an NGO information campaign finally spurred an international response in 1988. This helped build momentum for an international conference in Khartoum in March 1989 that led to the creation of OLS in April. This massive relief operation was coordinated by the UN out of Nairobi, Kenya, in order to organize aid delivery in Sudan among UN agencies. UNICEF was the lead agency and joined by the WFP and UNDP. The ICRC and various international NGOs completed the international team.

This UN-led OLS was a humanitarian "first" as until that point UN involvement in emergencies resulting from civil wars was extremely limited because of state sovereignty. While NGOs could more readily operate in cross-border efforts and directly talk with armed opposition groups, intergovernmental organizations were inhibited from working or negotiating directly with rebels. Member states resisted such a relationship because it lent legitimacy to belligerents— that is, they seemed on a par with the recognized government. In addition, either the government or the rebels were likely to be supported by either the West or the East, and hence it was important to avoid helping one side in the Cold War. The end of that struggle would open space for UN humanitarians to get involved on both sides of the conflict.[23]

OLS managed to gain agreement from not only the northern-based Sudanese government but also the leadership of the SPLA/M. One notable innovation was the establishment of "corridors of tranquility" along certain rivers and roads for guaranteed access in both the north and south. Before this agreement, aid agencies had usually been confined to working in refugee camps on the border of conflict zones. Now, however, both the government and nonstate belligerents agreed to create space in parts of an active war zone, which would become far more common after the end of the Cold War. Cross-border access for supplies brought directly from neighboring Kenya also was a breakthrough for the United Nations.

The situation became far more difficult after the June 1989 coup led by Colonel Omar Hassan Ahmad al-Bashir, who insisted on renegotiating the OLS agreement and demanded that most aid go to the north and that Khartoum clear all aid deliveries for the south. Thus, the historic cross-border agreement, while highlighting what can be achieved by broad diplomatic efforts, also demonstrates the difficulties of implementation on the ground when political circumstances change. This reality applies to any war zone but is especially problematic when a government comes to power and inherits an unfavorable agreement that appears to favor the armed opposition by facilitating aid.

Nicaragua and El Salvador

The refugee crisis in the 1980s resulting from the civil wars in Central America further illustrates the difficulty of maintaining neutrality in a highly politicized environment. Some agencies were openly biased and obtained funding from donor governments that shared their convictions. Such distinct political agendas for the region meant manipulation of the humanitarian situation by all sides for propaganda and military purposes. Progress in moving beyond the armed conflicts and the manipulation of aid would have to await the end of the Cold War, when the region was no longer one of the main flash points in the worldwide battle between Moscow and Washington.

The US government has been concerned about economic and security issues in what it considers to be its own "backyard" of Central America for over a century, a policy more formally known as the Monroe Doctrine. In the 1980s, a spike in Cold War tensions resulted with the election of President Ronald Reagan, who implemented a counter-policy in response to Soviet aiding of rebel groups. The so-called Reagan Doctrine was a counterpoint to the so-called Brezhnev Doctrine and sought to fight pro-Soviet left-wing governments around the world. Central America was far from the only battleground in this last act of the Cold War— we previously saw its manifestation in Afghanistan—but it was probably the most significant theater because Washington's direct military support was a major factor in violence that claimed the lives of tens of thousands and displaced hundreds of thousands more. US involvement mirrored Soviet unwillingness to tolerate an unfriendly government in its own backyard of Afghanistan.

First President Jimmy Carter and then Reagan provided military supplies and training to the Nicaraguan rebel movement known as the "Contras," which formed when a left-wing coalition overthrew the pro-American Somoza regime in 1979 and established the Soviet-friendly Sandinista government. Mostly coordinated through the the US Central Intelligence Agency (CIA), aid to the Contras amounted to tens of millions of dollars. Sometimes Washington provided support openly; but after Congressional prohibition in 1983, the Reagan administration continued to do so covertly. US government humanitarian aid also went exclusively to areas controlled by the Contras.

In El Salvador, the pro-US military government waged war throughout the 1980s against left-wing guerilla groups collectively known as the Farabundo Martí National Liberation Front (FMLN). Here, however, US military and financial support for the government was combined with propaganda attempts to discredit and undermine support for the

FMLN. Washington also withheld funding for humanitarian efforts in rebel-controlled territory.

The civil wars in Nicaragua and El Salvador led to substantial refugee flows (relative to their overall populations) into surrounding countries, especially Honduras, which borders both.[24] Similar to Afghan refugees in Pakistan, some of the camps were used as a haven for rebel groups crossing back over the border to fight. Also reminiscent is that the refugee camps became central to a propaganda war by the United States.

A massive increase in US military aid to Honduras during the 1980s encouraged the government to support the Contras and cooperate with their training and arming by the CIA on Honduran territory. Although this largely occurred outside the refugee camps, the Contras also operated openly within them. The camps also became useful to Washington in its media offensive to denigrate the Sandinistas and promote support for the Contras among the American people and Congress. Among other things, this effort involved tactics to increase the number of refugees that included encouraging Contra attacks in border areas of Nicaragua to provoke a harsh government response. Media coverage of fleeing Nicaraguans was then used to further tarnish the government's human rights record. The propaganda campaign was fuelled by the government's targeting of some native tribal groups, such as the Miskito, and destruction of their villages, which caused thousands more to flee to Honduras.

The refugee camps also stimulated private fund-raising in the United States. In addition to legitimate needs, rebel groups exaggerated the perceived problem by forcibly stopping people from returning home in order to attract more humanitarian funding. Rebels operating in the camps then diverted much of this aid. A further complication was Washington's sending "humanitarian" aid with the essential purpose of supplying its armed allies. Right-wing private groups, including conservative Christian charities in the United States, also sent non-military "humanitarian" supplies to aid the Contras.

Although such political smoke and mirrors diminished the credibility of fund-raising efforts by aid agencies in some quarters, it helped in others. Ironically in El Salvador, when Washington refused to fund efforts by UN agencies or NGOs operating in FMLN-controlled areas, for example, European NGOs and governments were motivated to mobilize even more resources for them. This discussion raises, as we hope the reader may already have concluded, the issue as to whether aid for combatants can ever actually be considered humanitarian, or whether all humanitarian aid is basically fungible (i.e., relieves a government or a belligerent from assisting populations in need and thereby frees up resources for war). Moreover, some aid agencies added fuel to the already highly combustible and politicized humanitarian fire by supporting only the Salvadoran rebels and civilians in areas controlled by them. Various volunteers who ostensibly came to work for agencies in Honduras were so ideologically committed that they often disappeared as soon as they arrived in order to work directly with FMLN rebels.

All of this greatly complicated the work of the UNHCR, MSF, and other relief agencies operating in the camps and elsewhere. The task of the UNHCR was also hindered by the fact that Honduras was not a signatory to the 1951 refugee convention. To maintain the government's cooperation, the UNHCR therefore felt obliged to temper its protests over military interference in the camps in order to retain access, however limited. It was also constrained by the political considerations of its primary financial backer, the US government, which was gaining propaganda value from the Nicaraguan camps as mentioned earlier.

Washington's absolute determination during the Cold War to undermine support for pro-Soviet governments and opposition movements in Central America greatly exacerbated an already difficult humanitarian challenge. The political commitment—or actively politicized stance—of many aid agencies as well as of individual staff also undermined humanitarian efforts. The traditional humanitarian stance of neutrality was often more fiction than fact. Interference—by rebels as well as by Honduran, Nicaraguan, Salvadoran, European, and American governments—served to create an even more complex and challenging environment for those who genuinely sought to give succor to and protect all civilians.

Tensions within the humanitarian enterprise and with states

Can we generalize about this second historical period when the traditional international humanitarian system prospered? Three trends of this period stand out: professionalization, politicization, and demilitarization.[25]

The first is the increasing number of organizations established and consolidated, or the bureaucratization of what Larry Minear calls "the humanitarian enterprise."[26] The creation of a dense network of organizations—many private and national societies and some other key international ones—began mostly in the West but then spread to other areas, particularly as newly independent states became parties to international law. Beyond improving the welfare of greater numbers of war victims, many aid agencies also matured as administrative structures, taking on a life of their own. They grew in size and resources and became more visible.

Institutions designed to respond to temporary crises in fact became permanent features of the international landscape. As mentioned above, the original need to resettle wartime refugees in Europe expanded to cover not only refugees from the Cold War on the continent but also from the rest of the planet. The UNHCR thus became a fixture of the UN system in 1951 and was further codified by its 1967 protocol.[27] Its mandate was not geared to a particular crisis but was couched generally to help those "who have crossed an international border because of a well-founded fear of persecution." Perhaps an even more telling case of a "temporary" humanitarian organization with great longevity is the UN Relief and Works Agency. This agency was designed to assist Palestinians displaced by the founding of Israel in 1948 and was supposed to last until Palestinians could be resettled in surrounding Arab states or until a political compromise with Israel could be reached that would provide for their return.[28] Over six decades later, the institution is now the UN's largest employer of local staff, and a fourth generation of Palestinians is being born under the watchful eye of this temporary body.

The second trend is politicization. By far the most striking aspect of the period covered by this chapter is the growing network of relationships among states, their militaries, and civilian members of the international humanitarian system. States are the parties to international agreements; and they authorize, recognize, and fund IGOs and in some cases NGOs to carry out humanitarian work. It is no surprise then that their activities also reflect the interests of donors. For example, the UNHCR was created because states feared the destabilizing impact of refugee flows in Europe following World War II. It was thus as much a reflection of state security interests and practical worries regarding multilateral burden-sharing as of humanitarian concerns. And it continued to serve a political purpose for the states that supported its operations while the Iron Curtain divided East from West, as it shielded, gave asylum to, and resettled those fleeing from communism to the West.[29]

Over time political leaders and relief workers have codified a set of norms that identify noncombatants and their rights to aid and protection. Neutrality, impartiality, and independence crystallized into guiding principles that became identified with the ICRC and then humanitarians more generally. The driving organizational idea was to avoid politics, be even-handed, and distribute assistance on the basis of need regardless of the location of victims (that is, on both sides of battle lines).

While it may be difficult for students of political science to understand, the international humanitarian system aspires to an absence of politics, with actors attempting to side-step concerns about partisanship and preferences in the administration of relief. The authority of aid agencies—even more than for other types of international organizations—is predicated on a myth that their activities serve the common interests of all humanity. "Politicization" nonetheless seems like an apt label because questions regarding who receives the primary benefits from the humanitarian delivery system in this second period, as it had been in the first, can often be explained by state interests and power.

The third general trend concerns the role of the military. In terms of human-made humanitarian disasters, the armed forces are primarily known for creating them through the force of destruction. Nonetheless, on many occasions the required humanitarian action was such that it could only be accomplished with the participation of these same armed forces. In the period immediately following World War II, for instance, the requirements were so large and the infrastructure so destroyed that the military command of the victorious Allied powers (the Supreme Headquarters Allied Expeditionary Force) was the only feasible vehicle for providing social services to refugees. Shortly thereafter the Allies would again use the armed forces to deliver aid past the Soviet blockade of East Germany during the Berlin Airlift.

The military's logistics cornucopia is impossible to duplicate easily or quickly in the private sector. While the armed forces thus remained a logistical fixture for certain humanitarian responses, this second period is characterized by a demilitarization of humanitarian action. The establishment of a host of specialized civilian organizations removed the onus that oftentimes fell on less-than-enthusiastic militaries, but this certainly did not mean that the task was to become cleaner and easier and less political. Michael Maren—who wrote about aid agencies after jobs in the Peace Corps, CRS, and the US Agency for International Development—tells us that "most American NGOs, just like the army and the marines, had been instruments of US foreign policy all along."[30]

Many humanitarians would dispute Maren's claim, but whenever the military was present as an occupying force, the model was "one of civilian humanitarian aid being subordinate to military authority," as Rachel McCleary tells us. The idea was that civilians would not interfere with military operations. "This setup remained the model of PVO [private voluntary organization]-military relations during and after World War II, the Korean War, and the Vietnam War. This model of civil-military relations began to change in the 1980s."[31] As we see later, this model has returned in major crises in Afghanistan and Iraq.

Conclusion: the end of the "golden years"

Despite the horrors and the challenges of the Cold War era, boundaries and ground rules for humanitarian action were relatively clear. The bad guys wore fatigues and carried guns, the good Samaritans wore sandals and succored victims caught in the cross-hairs of violence in wars. The United Nations, circumscribed by the sacrosanct sovereignty of its member states and severely constrained by the East–West rivalry, worked with governments and not with rebels. Neutrality and impartiality provided protection for those who sought to come to the rescue and save strangers.

Looking back from the perspective of the twenty-first century, David Rieff recommends a return to these "good old days," when the standard operating procedures of all humanitarians were the minimalist principles of the ICRC and its offshoot Médecins Sans Frontières.[32] However, it is worth repeating here Ian Smillie's views that respect for such principles has always been "patchy, weak or simply non-existent,"[33] and Hugo Slim's denial "that things used to be much better. Even a brief glance at humanitarian history shows this to be a rather eccentric view."[34] The reader will make his or her own judgment about the character of the 1945–89 years after we discuss the third historical period in the next two chapters.

In any case, these so-called golden years were initially followed by the mellowing of the Soviet Union and then the euphoria after the collapse of the Berlin Wall on 9 November 1989 and the implosion of the Soviet Union itself in December 1991. Humanitarians were freer to help, with the United Nations finally poised to act as its founders had intended. However, the warming of relations did not necessarily mean that humanitarian action was easily executed. As a Swahili proverb put it, "When the elephants make war, the grass suffers. When the elephants make love, the grass suffers."[35] For younger readers who recall mainly the civil wars and ghastly treatment of individuals and attacks on humanitarians in our times, the concerns of the late 1980s may seem very distant indeed.

4 The turbulent post–Cold War era
The "new" humanitarianism?

- **One picture ...**
- **Changing concepts of security**
- **Alternative approaches to ending violence**
- **Rights and responsibilities**
- **Conclusion: one step forward but how many back?**

The end of the Cold War marks the onset of the third historical period. Although the forces of destruction arguably had the greatest impact on expanding and reconfiguring the humanitarian system, the forces of salvation are an unheralded but equally important factor. Specifically, there was no denying the increase in deadly armed conflicts and mass suffering, but equally undeniable was the extent to which the response was guided not only by an attempt to treat the symptoms but also to eradicate the root causes of suffering and thus help bring about the kind of moral progress denied by the Cold War.

The conventional wisdom is that the end of the East–West rivalry was as earth-shaking for humanitarianism as it was for the world at large. There were certainly many substantial changes. But were they unprecedented and impossible to imagine? The quantitative and qualitative growth in the humanitarian enterprise discussed at the end of Chapter 1 provides some evidence in favor of the argument that the end of the Cold War introduced a completely new chapter in the life of humanitarianism. However, many of the processes identified by some observers as a consequence of the Cold War's end were already visible during the East–West conflict. History, context, and analysis can help us smooth off the edges of hyperbole.

This chapter explores what is truly "new" in humanitarianism and the broad historical factors that have given rise to these changes. We are particularly intrigued by the growing importance of the "civilian" as a category of protection. The notion that noncombatants need to be protected in war zones and the growing consensus of an international responsibility to provide them protection are remarkable developments.

The end of the East–West struggle led to tremendous optimism that the world would become as serious about peace as it had been about obliteration. However, the actual patterns of armed conflict provided a rude and bloody awakening. The ends of empires are invariably accompanied by a fight for political spoils and succession of power. The collapse of the Soviet Union offered no surprises in this regard. The Soviet empire's implosion led to fighting from Central Asia to the Caucasus and most famously and indirectly to the wars in the Balkans.

After decades during which secession was a taboo, the Union of Soviet Socialist Republics became Russia and 14 other successor states, and the Socialist Federal Republic of Yugoslavia ultimately spawned seven successor states. Suddenly, borders were no longer seen as sacrosanct elements of international stability but rather as arbitrary lines drawn by geographers and politicians. While the Soviet Union's collapse took place relatively peacefully, the former Yugoslavia came apart at the seams and led to major humanitarian crises in Croatia, Bosnia-Herzegovina, and finally Kosovo. As we see elsewhere, UN and North Atlantic Treaty Organization (NATO) involvement in the grizzly wars in the Balkans were critical events in the contemporary history of humanitarian action.

The end of the Cold War and the end to foreign aid by the Americans and the Soviets had domestic repercussions throughout the Third World. The worldwide competition between the two superpowers had provided a modest leverage in capitals where governments tried and often succeeded in extorting money from Washington or Moscow, or sometimes both. The foreign assistance that Third World leaders once used to maintain domestic order began to evaporate and, so too, did the peace. Somalia's post–Cold War collapse is a stark illustration of the role that superpower aid played in propping up weak states in the Third World. Somalia is probably best known for the US-led intervention in 1992 that was followed by the downing of Black-hawk helicopters and the dragging of US military personnel through the streets of Mogadishu, but the lead-up to that tragedy clearly illustrates why the East–West conflict provided a macabre leverage to many Third World governments.

What is often overlooked is that the back-and-forth among rivals in Somalia and elsewhere at the end of the Cold War was an extension of earlier uncertainties. The Scramble for Africa during the 1880s and 1890s had divided up the lands inhabited by the Somali people among the major powers. To Italy went southern Somalia, to Britain northern Somalia along the Gulf of Aden, to France the hinterlands of Tajoura; meanwhile

Ethiopia, which had gained the respect of the European powers with its decisive victory at Adwa, received the Ogaden region. British Somaliland became independent on 26 June 1960; the former Italian Somaliland followed suit five days later and the two territories united to form the Somali Republic, albeit within boundaries drawn up by Italy and Britain.

The Ogaden War (1977–78) is a stark illustration of the vagaries of the Cold War and the relevance of trading dance partners in an attempt to make the most of the competition between Washington and Moscow. This was a conventional armed conflict between Somalia and Ethiopia over the region of Ethiopia that Somalia claimed. During the war, the Soviet Union switched from supplying aid to Somalia to supporting Ethiopia, which had previously been backed by the United States until the Soviet-backed military Derg deposed Emperor Haile Selassie. This in turn prompted the United States to start supporting Somalia. The war ended with a truce after Somali forces retreated.

After years of military dictatorship, the country's importance in the East–West balance sheet evaporated. Instead of playing the superpowers off against each other to vie for rights to military bases, the rivalry between Moscow and Washington was replaced with indifference. Somalia subsequently descended into chaos and has remained without a central government since 1992, a political reality that is partly a result of international neglect.

The Somalia saga provides an introduction to an ongoing debate about whether there were, in fact, more emergencies than ever before or, instead, whether people were finally paying attention because they were no longer distracted by the Cold War's drama. We will let experts continue to parse the "objective" numbers and simply note that beginning in the 1990s there undoubtedly was greater interest in rescuing vulnerable populations. There were many reasons why it became more difficult for onlookers to do nothing in the face of preventable suffering. In short, the world was changing from the default position of "nothing can be done and horrors are an unfortunate fact of global life" toward a humanitarian imperative—the demand to act and to build the framework and machinery to make such action more likely and more effective.

Below we review these factors in some detail. This discussion sets the stage for the following chapter's analysis of the tensions between the international and the humanitarian systems.

One picture …

Many observers believe that growing public awareness of humanitarian calamities, made possible and plausible through real-time media coverage, helped feed the desire to do something. To be sure, there were important precursors to what eventually became dubbed the "CNN effect" or the "BBC effect." For the most part during the era of interstate warfare, the media mainly served state interests in gathering and maintaining the public's backing for war.

Media moguls of the nineteenth century found ready-made occasions to boost sales of newspapers by celebrating the joys of jingoism. For example, in 1897 as the Cuban population protested Spanish rule, US imperial ambitions manifested themselves through the likes of William Randolph Hearst's promise to "furnish the war."[1] While there is some doubt about whether he actually said that when a reporter suggested there was no war, mainstream US media certainly stoked frenzy for the 1898 Spanish–American War with slogans such as "Remember the *Maine.*" Inexpensive and widely available media fomented war then, just as the spread of radio captivated an even wider range of populations hungry for news of wars in the first part of the twentieth century.

The use of images can motivate or deter the political will required to enable military action; and with the development of real-time reporting, humanitarian suffering gave a new meaning to the old reporter's adage, "if it bleeds, it leads." Most famously, the haunting pictures with Biblical proportions of mass flight during the Ethiopian famine in the mid-1980s helped to stir not only public concern but also launch Band Aid/Live Aid.[2]

Since then, and especially in this third historical period, media coverage has been an important aspect of capturing the public's attention and fomenting international action. Without the media, at a minimum, appeals from humanitarians fall on deaf ears. In relationship to one of our main analytical prisms, salvation, John Hammock and Joel Charny described the media's treatment as "a scripted morality play" whose simplified images contribute to compassion fatigue and a failure to educate the public and politicians about root causes.[3] Milan Kundera's words in *The Book of Laughter and Forgetting* are poignant:

> the bloody massacre in Bangladesh quickly covered the memory of the Russian invasion of Czechoslovakia; the assassination of Allende drowned out the groans of Bangladesh; the war in the Sinai desert made people forget Allende; the Cambodian massacre made people forget Sinai; and so on and so forth, until ultimately everyone lets everyone be forgotten.[4]

None of this was lost on media-savvy aid workers, who understood the power of stark images and the necessity of controlling information; and thus they spent considerable energy cultivating contacts with reporters and journalists. A good public relations department and friends in the media would ensure visibility and thus increase the donations that make an organization thrive. CARE's miraculous growth in its early years, for example, owed much to a sophisticated and controlled presentation of its activities. Its acronym even became synonymous in the vernacular with relief packages to affected populations—the humanitarian marketing equivalent of "Xerox" becoming a synonym for "photocopy."[5] Oxfam's willingness to jump ahead of other aid agencies in famine-stricken Cambodia in the late 1970s was motivated in part to the inevitably good publicity that emanated from being the lone Western aid agency working in a post-genocide country.[6]

We need not debate exactly how many words a picture or a series of moving pictures is worth. It suffices to appreciate their essential contribution to public opinion and the public's willingness to support coming to the rescue.

Changing concepts of security

One reason for the growing visibility of humanitarian emergencies was because they were suddenly viewed as a security issue by major powers. Scholars, policymakers, and public intellectuals introduced a flood of new concepts to capture the messy, complicated, and bloody reality of contemporary war zones and their deadly consequences, and the necessary remedies.

Debate was widespread in various places, but nowhere more consequential than at the UN Security Council, the primary institutional home for discussing international responses to "threats to international peace and security." The accepted definition of that expression underwent considerable expansion after the dramatic collapse of the Soviet bloc.

During the Cold War, the council defined threats as disputes between states that might or had become militarized, conflicts involving the great powers, and general menaces to global stability.[7] The stand-off between East and West meant that few binding decisions (what distinguishes the council's from those of other UN bodies) were possible, especially regarding non-international (i.e., intra-state) wars. In particular, humanitarian disasters in and of themselves were insufficient for Security Council action.

After the end of the Cold War—and in reaction to the growing perception that domestic armed conflicts and civil wars were leaving hundreds of thousands of populations at risk, creating mass flight, and destabilizing entire regions—on numerous occasions the council identified humanitarian crises as threatening enough to require international action. Thus, it authorized coercive interventions on the grounds that war-induced disasters not only created massive human suffering but also imperiled regional and international security.[8]

Some talked about them as "new wars." Analytical works by Mary Kaldor and Mark Duffield, along with the more journalistic depictions by Robert Kaplan, popularized this term.[9] In what ways were they new? The modifier "new" does not necessarily indicate that an actual armed conflict began recently—indeed, many have dragged on for decades—but rather that the normal dynamics of war have changed.[10] Whether or not the dynamics of contemporary warfare are really all that new, they differ from archetypical interstate war in several aspects. The locus of war is domestic and not international. Contemporary wars are almost exclusively "civil," which explains why the ICRC's Additional Protocol II calls them "non-international." The term described not how these wars are fought, because they are anything except civil, but rather to contrast them with the more familiar international war. Although various forms of external support (including finance and arms sales as well as soldiers) complicate the simple designation of "domestic" or "internal," nonetheless we are referring to wars that involve sub-state and nonstate actors vying for control over a territory within the internationally agreed boundaries of a state.

A working definition of new wars is internal armed conflicts primarily waged by nonstate actors who subsist on illicit and parasitic economic behavior, use small arms and other low-technology hardware, and largely prey on and victimize civilians. One indication of this ugly reality is that the number of people internally displaced—and hence not protected by the international refugee regime—has grown steadily and stood at approximately 27 million in 2009, whereas the number of refugees has fallen and recently been at about half that number.[11]

The agents of war also differ. Whereas before there were regular armies that represented states and supposedly exercised a degree of discipline and demonstrated a degree of military professionalism, the new wars mobilize a motley assortment of combatants, including national armies, militias, paramilitaries, warlords, and child soldiers, many of whom have loyalties only to themselves and are highly undisciplined. Whereas conventional wars tended to be funded through domestic extraction—that is, taxation of various sorts—and international borrowing, actors in the new wars have relied on creative sources of funding, including selling commodities such as diamonds, giving rights to multinational corporations to harvest tropical timber, running drugs, and so on.

In the new wars, moreover, civilians are not an unfortunate casualty but rather are war's intended victims. Distinctions between civilian and combatant not only have no meaning, but those who fight war purposefully terrorize civilians, in part because the goal is to "cleanse" land and not just capture it. Although the widely cited ratio of 9:1 for war victims (civilians:combatants) is disputed, nonetheless most casualties of war are indeed civilians.[12] To accomplish their goals, combatants in the new wars do not need sophisticated, cutting edge technology, the sort of weaponry that shows up in recruiting advertisements for the US military, but rather such low-tech weapons as hand guns and machetes. The gruesome nature of these new wars also means that they are difficult to cover but also make for graphic images and headlines for those who manage to get access to the frontlines.

While this typology does not precisely fit any, and certainly not all, real-life armed conflicts, it enumerates the various facets of contemporary warfare that often come together and make life miserable for the denizens of war zones as well as for aid agencies. Although it was never easy being a humanitarian in armed conflict, the new wars truly are a nightmare. In the past, humanitarians had to worry about getting too close to the frontlines and negotiating access with representatives from states. Increasingly there are no frontlines and negotiating access is undertaken with groups who have no interest in the welfare of civilians—in fact, they benefit from the aid that these new wars attract. Such groups thus have every incentive to keep the killing, and the aid, coming. The principles and tactics that worked well in the past for humanitarians dealing with interstate wars may be less than ideal for the current generation of armed conflicts.[13]

Another concept that emerged from the embers of contemporary wars was "complex humanitarian emergency," defined as "conflict-related humanitarian disaster involving a high degree of breakdown and social dislocation and, reflecting this condition, requiring a system-wide aid response from the international community."[14] Such emergencies are characterized by a combustible mixture of state failure, refugee flight, militias, warrior refugees, and populations at risk from violence, disease, and hunger. They created a demand for new sorts of interventions and conflict-management tools. Relief agencies attempting to distribute food, water, and medicine in war zones were frequently forced to bargain with militias, warlords, and hoodlums for access to populations in need. In situations of extreme violence and lawlessness, they often lobbied foreign governments and the United Nations to consider authorizing military protection forces that could double as bodyguards and relief distributors.

Around this same time analysts and practitioners began articulating the concept of "human security," perhaps the most radical shift in thinking on peace and conflict prevention since the UN's establishment.[15] The notion was first presented in the *Human Development Report 1994*: "The concept of security has for too long been interpreted narrowly: as security of territory from external aggression, or as protection of national interests in foreign policy or as global security from the threat of a nuclear holocaust. It has been related more to nation states than to people."[16] At bottom, this report argued for new thinking about the protection of people from a diversity of threats to their life and dignity. The expanded threats include economic security as well as the security of food, health, environment, and community. The key features of human security are people-centered, universal, interdependent, and easier to ensure through early prevention than through later intervention.

Why was this of interest to humanitarians? From the seventeenth to the end of the twentieth century, as we have seen, states had been the main focus of war and of humanitarian action. Suddenly the basic concern of humanitarians with the welfare of people coincided with the emphasis in UN security rhetoric more generally—moving from preoccupation with state security toward a refocusing on the security needs and aspirations of human beings.

Alternative approaches to ending violence

After 1989, scholars and practitioners also began making new kinds of connections between domestic and international order. Instead of the prevailing wisdom that international order is best preserved through superior firepower, deterrence, and sovereignty, policymakers as well as academics began drawing new kinds of maps that linked domestic processes with international security. Domestic instability and conflict did not respect state boundaries; the repercussions could not be easily contained at the edge of a state's borders. At first policymakers were impressed by the magnitude of refugee flows, international displacement, and other forces of instability spawned from domestic conflict; and after 2001 they also emphasized the role of failed states as mass producers of global terrorism. Consequently, domestic instability became ipso facto a matter of international peace and security; and the international community of states was stimulated to devise alternative solutions to extinguish the breeding grounds for terrorists.

Among the various responses to ending violence, two are particularly important because of their enduring significance. One is that democratization and economic liberalization are widely considered to be solutions. If authoritarianism, lack of economic opportunities, and human rights violations are the root causes of violence, then democratic transition, market reform, and establishing the rule of law are the remedies. International actors can indeed play a particularly important role in nurturing the forces of legitimacy, peace, and stability; and a cottage industry of post-conflict peace-building emerged as a result.[17]

Intergovernmental organizations promote values of democratization and economic liberalization. State-building expertise and investment resources are available for feeble and failing states through UN agencies.[18] The results are mixed, but numerous states and territories have received assistance in the last 20 years, including Bosnia and Herzegovina, Cambodia, the Democratic Republic of the Congo, El Salvador, Kosovo, Mozambique, Nicaragua, Sierra Leone, and East Timor.

In addition to states from the global North, IGOs from the UN system and the Bretton Woods institutions along with international NGOs have led the way in implementing liberalism as the only acceptable model for contemporary state-building. On the economic side, the private sector and Washington-based financial institutions are at the forefront of economic policymaking while the government's role is largely confined to the maintenance of macroeconomic stability. As a condition for loans from the International Monetary Fund (IMF) and World Bank, states are required to respect market mechanisms. In addition to fiscal austerity and privatization, the neoliberal package includes trade liberalization and thus participation in the World Trade Organization. Since the 1990s, structural adjustment programs have become overtly political, requiring respect for "good governance"—including ensuring the rule of law, transparency, accountability, and reducing government corruption.[19]

Northern states, IGOs, and NGOs have also promoted political liberalization and democratization with such mechanisms as human rights monitoring and reporting and election monitoring and endorsement. Roland Paris reminds us, however, of the dangers when formal procedural democracy geared toward elections trumps more thoroughgoing structural change in countries recovering from armed conflict.[20] At the extreme, the UN has actually endorsed military intervention for democratic regime change, such as that of the threatened US-led invasion of Haiti in 1994 in Security Council resolution 940, and of Kosovo retroactively in 1999 in resolution 1244.

Regardless of whether or not peace-building resolves or perpetuates conflict, there is little doubt that international actors are beginning to map in new ways the possibilities for peace, the second related and enduring response to the rise of new security threats. Here we want to emphasize how different international bodies are thinking about addressing the root causes of conflict. Some "learning" results from the fact that complex humanitarian emergencies attracted a range of nongovernmental organizations to become more involved in the same space.[21] Relief agencies delivering emergency assistance, human rights organizations aspiring to protect human rights and create a rule of law, and development agencies sponsoring sustainable growth began to interact on the same crowded stage and to take responsibility for the same populations. Growing interactions encouraged relief–rights–development links within humanitarian discourse that became tied to the construction of modern, legitimate, democratic states.[22] As various international actors began to think about the causes of and solutions to disasters, they situated their arguments under a humanitarian rubric that was tied to a wider range of desirable policy changes and practices. Humanitarianism became a central part of the new security agenda.

Rights and responsibilities

Alongside these changes in security, there were several breakthroughs in the ethics of international rights and responsibilities. Perhaps best known was the growing internationalization and institutionalization of human rights. As noted, after World War II the international community of states began to construct various kinds of legal regimes, but by and large they were ignored. Overtime, human rights became an increasingly important part of the international landscape, and then with the end of the Cold War the discourse of rights was everywhere. Everyone seemed to be part of the human rights congregation, almost to the point that it became the new religion albeit with many sinners.

Although there were many states that were not so accepting of the language of human rights, including those who believed that it was nothing more than the new ideology for the powerful West, it is important to note that humanitarians had their own reservations. The logic of relief and the logic of rights share some important elements: they place front and center the individual and humanity; and they are concerned with empowering victims, the weak, and the powerless.[23] That said, they also demonstrate some serious divisions because relief agencies will nearly always privilege survival over freedom, while the human rights community is willing, at times, to use relief as an instrument to foster rights. The difference in priorities is most evident when rights-oriented agencies are willing to make relief conditional on the observance of human rights standards, a move that many relief agencies view as nearly incomprehensible.[24] In any event, the fast-growing human rights agenda pulled humanitarianism from the margins toward the center of the international public policy agenda. And many relief agencies increasingly adopted the language of rights and were glad to ride its coat-tails.[25]

The UN's universal membership and global network of field offices made it a logical coordinator for humanitarian responses. Whereas once human rights were relegated to Geneva's UN bureaucracies and NGO watchdogs, the Security Council in this period became more deeply involved in interpreting, protecting, promoting, and monitoring fundamental rights. The respect for human rights became an essential component of several UN peacekeeping operations, most notably in what had been the Cold War flashpoints of Central America—El Salvador, Nicaragua, and Guatemala. In Rwanda and Haiti, human rights missions were deployed simultaneously with peacekeeping operations. The results of these operational experiments were mixed, certainly. However, it remains noteworthy that human rights became central on the Security Council's agenda and part of an expanded definition of what constitutes a legitimate threat to international peace and security.

There also were important changes in the meaning of state sovereignty. There was a shift from negative to positive sovereignty.[26] Whereas once their legitimacy appeared to have near-divine origins, now it was dependent on states' possessing such characteristics as the rule of law, markets, and democratic principles. These developments created a normative space for external intervention and encouraged a growing range of actors to expand their assistance activities; in some cases they aimed to provide immediate relief during armed conflicts, and in others to eliminate the root causes of war and create legitimate states. Regardless of the rationale, the new normative environment greased the tracks for more wide-ranging interventions.[27] Sovereignty was no longer enough; and it no longer provided a safe haven for serial violators of human rights.

The revolution in rights and sovereignty had a decisive impact on the growing willingness to deploy military force for human protection purposes—that is, what we encountered earlier under the guise of "humanitarian intervention."[28] The Cold War Security Council occasionally acknowledged the existence of humanitarian issues, but both rhetorical and financial support was trivial in comparison with the period after 1989. No council resolution mentioned the humanitarian dimensions of any conflict from 1945 until the Arab–Israeli war of 1967, and the first mention of the ICRC was not until 1978.[29] In the 1970s and 1980s, "the Security Council gave humanitarian aspects of armed conflict limited priority … but the early nineteen-nineties can be seen as a watershed."[30]

Not only was the Security Council undergoing a military rebirth after being comatose during the Cold War, but its resolutions suddenly also contained repeated references to humanitarian crises as threats to international peace and security, the trigger for council action. Resolution 792 in December 1992 broke all records in making 18 references to the "H" word in authorizing US-led action in Somalia. There seemed to be no turning back from humanitarianism as a catalyst for international attention and sometimes action.

The Security Council's growing involvement in the internal affairs of states, and justification for that involvement on humanitarian grounds, signaled a shift in parsing the meaning of sovereignty. Once beyond reproach, states were now expected to respect their own citizens' sovereignty as much as that of their neighbors'. Moreover, they faced possible sanctions if they behaved otherwise. State sovereignty became more conditional and implied dual contracts between the state and its society (internal) as well as among states (international).

What happened when states broke these contracts? Some members of the international community of states began to assert that they had at least a responsibility and perhaps a right, although not an obligation or duty, to step into the breach and protect vulnerable populations. Although there were whispers of an international legal obligation to protect civilians, most famously if the terms of the 1948 genocide convention were breached, the momentum for actually enforcing it was largely a post–Cold War phenomenon.

Various statements, documents, events, and forces opened up normative and operational space for kinds of humanitarian intervention, but several moments were particularly influential because they helped to articulate and legitimate such a claim. In the late 1980s and early 1990s, Francis M. Deng and Roberta Cohen formulated the concept "sovereignty as responsibility" to help generate support for international action to aid and protect internally displaced persons (IDPs).[31] In addition to Deng and Cohen's conceptual work, two council resolutions were ground-breaking in this period: resolution 678, which authorized the protection of civilians in northern Iraq after the Gulf War, and resolution 794, which authorized military intervention by US-led forces to provide humanitarian assistance to war victims in Somalia. Together these signaled that "sovereignty was no longer sacrosanct."[32] In Iraq, it was set aside while in Somalia it had disappeared.

As a consequence of interventions undertaken (Kosovo and East Timor) and not undertaken (Rwanda), in 1999 Secretary-General Kofi Annan articulated "two sovereignties."[33] The subsequent diplomatic uproar over the relative weights of individual versus state sovereignty led to the formation of the International Commission on Intervention and State Sovereignty,[34] whose final report argued that when states cannot or will not protect their populations, or themselves are actively abusing them, then the international community of states should assume the "responsibility to protect."

Since its emergence as the subject and title of the 2001 ICISS report, the responsibility to protect (now commonly abbreviated to "R2P") has shaped international conversations and decisions about how the international community of states should respond to the most egregious violations of human rights and the most conscience-shocking humanitarian disasters. Given R2P's declared goal to change the terms of discourse toward a non-contested humanitarianism, how far is it presently from the status of an international norm? How long can a norm be described as "emerging" before it truly "has emerged"?

R2P attempts to move beyond the counterproductive and toxic label of "humanitarian intervention." Since the international response in northern Iraq in 1991, this moniker often led to largely circular tirades about the agency, timing, legitimacy, means, circumstances, and advisability of using military force to protect human beings.

The central normative tenet of the responsibility to protect, as envisaged first in the 2001 ICISS report and embraced later by over 150 heads of state and government at the UN's 2005 World Summit,[35] is that state sovereignty is contingent and not absolute. After centuries of largely looking the other way, sovereignty no longer provided a license for mass murder. Each state has a responsibility to protect its own citizens from mass killings and other gross violations of their rights. If a state, however, is unable or unwilling to exercise its responsibility, or actually is the perpetrator of mass atrocities, its sovereignty is abrogated. Meanwhile the responsibility to protect devolves to the international community of states, ideally acting through the UN Security Council.

As mentioned earlier, the double responsibility in this framework—internal and external—draws upon earlier work by Francis Deng and Roberta Cohen on sovereignty as responsibility. Hence, both the 2001 ICISS report and the *World Summit Outcome Document* moved away from humanitarian intervention as a "right" (that is, one that could be deployed and perhaps manipulated without consistent adherence to rigorous standards and accepted principles). Both emphasized the need—indeed, the responsibility—for the international community of states, embodied by the United Nations and mandated since its creation to deliver "freedom from fear"—to do everything possible to prevent mass atrocities. Deploying military force is an option after alternatives have been considered and have patently failed to end mass atrocities.

Military intervention to protect the vulnerable is further restricted, in the summit's language, only to cases of "genocide, war crimes, ethnic cleansing and crimes against humanity." The shorthand for these four is "mass atrocity crimes."

Using the military *in extremis* to save strangers was the lynch-pin for the debate growing especially from Rwanda (doing too little too late) and Kosovo (according to some, doing too much too soon). However, the R2P agenda comprises more complex and subtle responses to mass atrocities than merely the use of overwhelming military force to halt them after they have begun. Responses range from prevention to post-conflict rebuilding in order to protect civilians at risk.[36] While participants at the World Summit left aside post-conflict peace-building and emphasized prevention and reaction, the full spectrum of prevention, reaction, and rebuilding are an essential part of the original ICISS conceptualization of the responsibility to protect.

The integrity of the concept suffers, in our view, when diluted. It is important to ensure that R2P does not become synonymous with everything that the United Nations does. In addition to reacting in the eye of the storm and halting mass atrocity crimes, the value added of R2P consists of proximate prevention and proximate peace-building— that is, efforts to move back from the brink of atrocities that have yet to become widespread or efforts after mass atrocity crimes to ensure that they do not recur. R2P is above all about taking timely preventive action, about identifying situations that are capable of deteriorating into mass atrocities and bringing to bear diplomatic, legal, economic, and military pressure in a prudent fashion to prevent or end the suffering and death resulting from mass atrocities. International action is required long before the only option remaining is the US Army's 82nd Airborne Division; and additional commitments to help mend societies after deploying outside military forces are also necessary.

To repeat, the responsibility to protect is also not about the protection of everyone from everything. The broadening of perspectives has opened the floodgates to an overflow of appeals to address too many problems. For example, part of the political support at the World Summit reflected an understandable but erroneous desire to use R2P to mobilize more support for root-cause prevention, or investments in economic and social development. As bureaucrats invariably seek justifications for pet projects, we run the risk that there is nothing that may not figure on the R2P agenda. It is emotionally tempting and even morally compelling to say that we have a responsibility to protect people from HIV/AIDS and small arms, or the Inuit from global warming. However, if R2P means everything, it amounts to nothing. And the international community of states will once again stand by in impotent silence when machine guns or machetes result in mass murder because there is no operationally viable universal norm to call upon, no narrow and specific-purpose mechanism of protection to implement rapidly and effectively.

Yet the responsibility to protect also should not be viewed too narrowly. It is not, and this cannot be said too frequently, *only* about the use of military force. R2P is not a synonym for "humanitarian intervention," although proponents sometimes lapse into this language. This task is especially pertinent after Washington's and London's rhetoric disingenuously morphed into a vague "humanitarian" justification for the war in Iraq when weapons of mass destruction and links to Al Qaeda proved non-existent. The Iraq war was almost a conversation stopper for R2P as critics looked askance upon any humanitarian justification for military force. In the eyes of harsh critics of American adventurism, a humanitarian Trojan horse remained a Trojan horse for imperial meddling, nonetheless.

With these caveats, readers should still be aware that the R2P norm breaks new ground in ways to think about coming to the rescue. In addition to the usual attributes of a sovereign state that students encounter in international relations and law courses and in the 1933 Montevideo Convention—people, authority, territory, and independence—there is another: a modicum of respect for basic human rights. The traditional emphasis on privileges for sovereigns has made room for modest responsibilities for them as well. Moreover, when a state is unable or manifestly unwilling to protect the rights of its population—and especially when it is the perpetrator of abuse—that state temporarily loses its sovereignty along with the accompanying right of non-intervention. In brief, the traditional rule of non-interference in the internal affairs of other countries no longer applies in the face of mass atrocities.

Moreover, ICISS turned the language of humanitarian intervention on its head and moved away from that detested in significant parts of the global South. The merits of particular situations should be evaluated rather than blindly blessed as "humanitarian." For anyone familiar with the number of sins justified by the use of that adjective during colonization, this change marked a profound shift away from the rights of outsiders to intervene and toward the rights of populations at risk to assistance and protection and the responsibility of outsiders to help.

In what Gareth Evans estimates to be "a blink of the eye in the history of ideas,"[37] developments since the release of the ICISS report in December 2001 suggest that R2P has moved from the prose and passion of an international commission's published report toward being a mainstay of international public policy. It also has substantial potential to evolve further in customary international law and to contribute to ongoing conversations about the responsibilities of states as legitimate, rather than rogue, sovereigns. In 2004, the UN's High-level Panel on Threats, Challenges and Change issued *A More Secure World: Our Shared Responsibility*, which supported "the emerging norm that there is a collective international responsibility to protect."[38] Former UN secretary-general Kofi Annan endorsed it in his 2005 report, *In Larger Freedom*.[39] A significant normative advance came in September 2005, when heads of state unanimously supported the responsibility to protect in paragraphs 138 and 139 of the *World Summit Outcome Document*. In addition to the official blessing by the UN General Assembly in October 2006, the Security Council made specific references to R2P on two occasions: the April 2006 resolution 1674 on the protection of civilians in armed conflict expressly "reaffirms the provisions of paragraphs 138 and 139," and the August 2006 resolution 1706 on Darfur, which was the first to link R2P to a particular conflict.

Since that time the current UN secretary-general, Ban Ki-moon, appointed a full-time special adviser for the prevention of genocide (Francis M. Deng) and special adviser tasked with promoting R2P (Edward C. Luck). He has referred to the implementation of R2P as one of his priorities, and he released *Implementing the Responsibility to Protect* in January 2009. Ban details a "three pillar" approach for implementing R2P, which includes the protection responsibilities of individual states, international assistance and capacity-building, and timely and decisive international responses.[40]

The UN General Assembly interactive dialogue in late July 2009 was another step in R2P's normative journey although hardly what Secretary-General Ban described as "a watershed."[41] The states members of the Group of Friends of the Responsibility to Protect in New York, the UN special adviser, and civil society actively forged a wider constituency on the issue and mobilized around the secretary-general's report.[42] They thus picked up the mantle from previous "norm entrepreneurs" by drawing upon successful recent campaigns to forge wider constituencies for such issues as banning landmines and establishing the International Criminal Court (ICC).

Initially, many observers feared that the debate would produce a resolution deliberately diluting the September 2005 commitment. The fears about normative backpedaling seemed concrete enough; the *Economist* described opponents who "have been busily sharpening their knives."[43] Critics painted R2P in imperialistic colors. The Nicaraguan president of the General Assembly, Father Miguel d'Escoto Brockmann, called it "redecorated colonialism" and suggested "a more accurate name for R2P would be the right to intervene."[44]

However, R2P-naysayers were deeply disappointed by the actual debate's tone and the discernible shift from antipathy to wider public acceptance of this emerging norm.[45] Of course, countries that had suffered terrible atrocities made rousing pleas to strengthen and implement R2P—for example, Bosnia, East Timor, Guatemala, Rwanda, and Sierra Leone. Also, a wide variety of countries from the global South such as Chile and South Korea and the entire West expressed their firm support. The widening consensus was less expected. A close reading of remarks by diplomats from 92 countries and 2 observers who addressed the plenary showed scant support for undermining R2P. Only Venezuela directly questioned the 2005 World Summit agreement, and only four countries expressed opposition and sought to roll back the earlier consensus: Cuba, Nicaragua, Sudan, and Venezuela. Supportive remarks also came from major regional powers that had previously been reticent or even hostile—including Brazil, India, Japan, Nigeria, and South Africa. Understandably, many countries expressed concerns about implementation, particularly regarding thresholds and inconsistency.

Thus, despite disagreement and contestation, the General Assembly showed considerably more support for implementing the earlier 2005 consensus than for moving backward. In September 2009 and again in December 2010, its resolutions 63/208 and 64/245 clearly indicated widespread support across regions. Ramesh Thakur and Thomas G. Weiss are not exaggerating when they write that the cumulative impact is "the most dramatic normative development of our time."[46]

A different type of naysayer is found among supporters of humanitarian action who find that the responsibility to protect has the potential to backfire because of the problem of moral hazard. Alan Kuperman, for instance, is one of the contrarians who has argued that the expectation of benefiting from possible outside intervention—and he includes sanctions, embargoes, judicial pursuit, and military force—emboldens sub-state groups of rebels either to launch or continue fighting.[47] We certainly know of instances when international involvement has affected the calculations of local militias and elites, even causing them to take action that perhaps had the effect, intended and unintended, of prolonging the violence.

But does this mean that robust humanitarianism is destined to constitute a moral hazard? Perhaps there would be a problem if there were for humanitarians the sort of insurance policy that allows banks to be reckless with other peoples' money. However, there is no such global life insurance policy, and combatants know this. Moreover, the opposite problem is probably more likely: everyone knows that talk is cheap in international diplomacy. If the ICC's issuing an arrest warrant for Sudanese president Omar al-Bashir is as empty a threat as the use of outside military force to halt the slow-motion genocide in Darfur, then it is not so much moral hazard that is the problem but rather collective spinelessness. Lastly, the moral hazard argument, if taken seriously, could lead to the conclusion that pledging to do nothing is the right thing, which would certainly have human consequences and potentially give perpetrators a license to kill.

Conclusion: one step forward but how many back?

R2P is at the beginning of a long, normative journey. As with all humanitarian initiatives—beginning with the Geneva Conventions almost 150 years ago—considerable time always elapses before emerging norms stimulate routine change and compliance. It is hard to disagree with David Rieff that "there is considerable evidence of changing norms, though not, of course, changing facts on the ground."[48] Yet, should we despair completely about effective international action in the face of conscience-shocking horrors? Some optimism should result because the responsibility to protect does not set the foreign policy bar impossibly high. R2P is about halting mass atrocities, not establishing Immanuel Kant's perpetual peace on earth. It is concerned with the clearest moral and legal cases.

Surely it's not quixotic to say no more Holocausts and Rwandas— and to mean it? Or is it? Alas, answers to those questions are less clear than R2P proponents would like, as we see in the next chapter.

5 Turbulent humanitarianism since 1989

Rhetoric meets reality

- **Politics all the way down**
- **Failing responsibilities**
- **What is "new" about the new humanitarianism?**
- **Conclusion: unlimited ambitions—and whose?**

The preceding chapter spelled out the important changes in thinking and practice in the so-called new humanitarianism. Here, we turn to the growing tensions between the international and the humanitarian systems—that is, one system driven by the logic of vital state interests versus another driven by the logic of humanity. Who bends to whose will?

The growth of humanitarianism is associated with the humanization of politics while humanitarianism itself is becoming more political. The growing role of states, as we hope to have made clear by now, is not making its maiden appearance with the end of the Cold War but rather has always been a feature of humanitarian action. Examining global developments throughout this chapter helps us begin to address the central question: Is anything really new under the sun? Our answer is, equivocally, both "yes" and "no."

Politics all the way down

Considerable controversy continues about the relationship between the expanding agenda of international peace and security, humanitarianism, and state interests. If something appears to be too good to be true, it probably is—and growing state interest in humanitarian action followed this basic axiom. While it would be overly cynical to assert that the only reason they were interested in the suffering of others was self-interest, it would also be unspeakably naïve to suggest that states had changed their stripes after centuries of interjecting politics and power into every facet of global life. The proverbial bottom line was that while states were facilitating the expansion of humanitarian action, they were doing so in a manner that left a trail of state interests.

However present state interests, governments were undeniably more open to humanitarian considerations. Why? Arguably they recalculated the relationship between interests and the potential impacts of humanitarian disasters in an increasingly interconnected world. Complex humanitarian emergencies had regional and sometimes international consequences, which reinforced the view that there was a close relationship between domestic and international order. Michael Ignatieff, for one, pointed to "bad neighborhoods" such as Afghanistan and Sudan, which offered fertile soil for international terrorists. For instance, such areas were breeding grounds for those who perpetrated the attacks on US embassies in East Africa in 1998, the *U.S.S. Cole* in Yemen in 2000, and US soil in Pennsylvania, New York, and Washington, DC, in September 2001.[1] It became clear that failed states were a threat not only to themselves but also to others. Hence international actors could not ignore them and, indeed, had a vested interest in "saving" them.[2]

The claimed relationship between security and humanitarianism has been especially evident since 9/11. States also began discovering ways in which their security interests had an interface with humanitarian action. In the post-9/11 global war on terror—in March 2009 relabeled "overseas contingency operation" by the US Defense Department—counterterrorism and humanitarianism, at least according to the United States and other major Western powers, have become partners. With failed states as sanctuaries and staging platforms for terrorists, humanitarian organizations can become part of wider "hearts and minds" campaigns, attempting to convince local populations of the goodness of armies invading in the name of stability and freedom. In his now infamous words, US secretary of state Colin Powell told a gathering of private aid agencies that "just as surely as our diplomats and military, American NGOs are out there [in Afghanistan] serving and sacrificing on the frontlines of freedom. NGOs are such a force multiplier for us, such an important part of our combat team."[3] Such logic was hardly unusual, but Powell's straightforward billing was far clearer than the packaging from some of his predecessors. Humanitarians were force multipliers after World War II as well as in Korea, Vietnam (and elsewhere in Southeast Asia), Afghanistan, and Central America. However, no prior secretary of state thought that NGOs were important enough to address at a gathering and say clearly and without apology what everyone already knew.

States also discovered that humanitarian action could avoid or postpone more costly political decisions and actions. Michael Ignatieff explains why: "Coverage of humanitarian assistance allows the West the illusion that it is doing something; in this way, coverage becomes an alternative to more serious political engagement." He continues that the real story is thus one of disengagement "while the moral lullaby we allow our humanitarian consciences to sing is that we are coming closer and closer."[4] Former US president Theodore Roosevelt responded in a similar way to the decision by one of his successors, Woodrow Wilson, to steer clear of the 1915 Armenian genocide. "To allow the Turks to massacre the Armenians," he said, "and then solicit permission to help the survivors and then to allege the fact that we are helping the survivors as a reason why we should not follow the only policy that will permanently put a stop to such massacres is both foolish and odious."[5]

The fig leaves of the 1990s were labeled a "humanitarian alibi" by frustrated aid workers who felt that they were being manipulated by states. Former UN high commissioner for refugees Sadako Ogata, for one, became an outspoken opponent of such contrivances: "There are no humanitarian solutions to humanitarian problems."[6] Mark Duffield has pointed out that viewing armed conflicts as having local causes— ethnicity, tribalism, and religion—serves a political purpose of legitimating a purely humanitarian response; it is easier then to underplay the role of exogenous forces including trade, colonialism, and inequality.[7] One need not agree with Duffield, who views humanitarian action as a means to maintain Western hegemony, in order to appreciate the reasons that it is easier to respond with humanitarian salve rather than intervene militarily or economically to halt let alone address the root local or international causes of war and violence.

Ogata once described herself as "the desk officer for the former Yugoslavia" because the major powers had authorized the UNHCR to deliver vast amounts of humanitarian relief in Bosnia, in part to relieve the growing pressure for a military intervention. Regardless of whether or not states possessed the right motives, they afforded new opportunities for relief and protection in areas that formerly had been largely off-limits for civilian humanitarians. Yet to the extent that it became a substitute for politics and a sop to hopeful publics, aid could, according to Alex de Waal, lead "Western governments and donating publics to be deluded into believing the fairy tale that their aid can solve profound political problems, when it cannot."[8]

Because they were more interested in humanitarianism, they were providing more money. Although private contributions increased, they paled in comparison to official assistance. We should briefly reiterate some data from Chapter 1. Between 1990 and 2000 aid levels rose from just over $2 billion to almost $6 billion, a near threefold increase; and another tripling occurred by 2008 to some $18 billion. Moreover, as a percentage of official development assistance, humanitarian aid rose from an average of around 6 percent in the early 1990s to somewhere between 7.5 and 10 percent over the last decade.

A few donors were responsible for much of this increase, and they also now comprise an oligopoly. Outlays by the United States as the remaining superpower exceeded the total assistance of the next 12 largest Western donors. The second largest donor is the European Community Humanitarian Organization, followed by the United Kingdom, several European countries, Canada, and Japan. While some diversification has taken place, the vast bulk of humanitarian resources emanates from the West.

The bilateralization of aid and earmarking of funds not only channeled efforts by individual agencies but also led to new trends in aid allocations. Again, we should recall the statistics from the initial discussion of these "essentials." Multilateral aid is often considered superior because technically it is defined as aid handed over to intergovernmental organizations and is not earmarked so that these organizations determine how the money is spent. In contrast to multilateral aid, bilateral aid is earmarked, which means that the donor state dictates to funding recipients how the money is to be spent, including specifying a particular geographic region or even pet projects to benefit constituents back home.

The increase in bilateralism and earmarking since the 1980s has been striking. From 45 percent of the total aid in 1988 that was multilateral, the average dropped to 25 percent by the mid-1990s and continued downward to 11 percent in 2007. State interests, rather than the principle of relief based on need, increasingly drives funding decisions. In general, while there are more humanitarian dollars and euros than ever before, they are controlled by fewer donors that are more inclined to impose conditions and direct aid toward their own priorities, thereby undermining impartiality. A several-tiered system means that the least fortunate often get the least attention. In response to the politicization of priorities, humanitarian organizations entered into a dialogue with the principal donors to try and establish more impartial standards, and the result was the Good Donorship Initiative (GDI).[9]

State interests affected the pattern of giving—or rather, whose suffering matters. While humanitarians speak of their practice of giving based on need, states will use their interests to determine whose needs matter—and they have the power to get their way. Because most humanitarian organizations are highly dependent on government funding, states can use this resource dependence to their advantage. Donors can make threats to influence how agencies behave. In 2003, US Agency for International Development administrator Andrew Natsios was rumored to have told humanitarian organizations operating in Iraq that they were obligated to show the American flag if they were recipients of US funding. If they refused to do so, he warned them that they could be replaced.[10] One NGO official captured Washington's message: "play the tune or 'they'll take you out of the band.'"[11] It turns out the story was mere rumor and the statement never occurred, but that it was believed and reported widely says something about the climate of the times and the collective state of mind of aid agencies.

The 1990s were unprecedented to the extent that states attempted to impose their agendas on agencies.[12] States began introducing mechanisms that were intended to control their "implementing partners." Although such devices did not necessarily compel agencies to act in ways that they believed were antagonistic to their interests or principles, frequently they did.[13]

Most famously, NATO in Kosovo and the United States in Afghanistan insisted on coordinating humanitarian action.[14] Although they justified their coordination role on the grounds that it would improve the effectiveness of the overall relief effort, self-interested reasons provide a more accurate explanation. In order to sell the war at home, the combatants wanted the favorable publicity that accompanied media coverage of their delivering food to and building shelters for displaced populations. It also would help them win the "hearts and minds" campaign that was integral to the war effort.

States also became more desirous of seeing for themselves what was occurring in the field. Toward that end, they began sending representatives directly into the field to provide first-hand accounts of activities and hence developing the capacity for independent needs assessments and strategic analyses. An immediate consequence was that aid agencies no longer benefited from having privileged and highly authoritative information. Whereas once aid agencies possessed private information and were the recognized experts on the basis of their first-hand and privileged knowledge, the growing presence of governmental officials meant that humanitarians lost their monopoly position or at least comparative informational advantage. Because NGO authority comes from their practical experience in the trenches, this development undermined their leverage.[15]

Aid agencies can be as—if not more—concerned with their survival as they are with the survival of others. Humanitarian organizations might want to help others survive, but they also care about their own well-being—after all, the ultimate welfare of others is predicated on humanitarians' own survival and the resources available. Partially as a result of funding, the population of aid agencies has exploded over the last two decades. Whether the marketplace literally unleashes what two colleagues have called a "scramble" for monies,[16] an environment of scarce resources invariably creates a competitive drive for status, power, and authority.

Most agencies do not have the luxury of opting out of the scramble for what the marketplace offers. The debate is not about whether to participate in the market but to what extent. Dining with the devil became a foregone conclusion, but whether their spoons were long enough and exactly how they rationalized such repasts varied agency by agency. The humanitarian expansion into activities following a disaster may seem logical and even desirable to ensure continuity between an emergency and what follows. It can also be seen, more cynically, as a way to expand an institution, as Michael Maren tells us: "Few NGOs have ever seen a contract they didn't like, or a problem they didn't believe they could solve."[17] In general, the more states were willing to use funding to further their political interests, the more NGOs were willing to do what it takes to keep on the good side of those with the money.

Moreover, humanitarian organizations were being coordinated by one of the parties to the conflict, compromising their neutrality and independence. A major controversy in this regard was the willingness of aid agencies to align themselves with the United States in Afghanistan and Iraq, which also was one of the causes behind the growing perception that aid workers were no longer shielded while providing help in war zones.

Failing responsibilities

Perhaps the most glaring and depressing example of the logic of state interests trumping the logic of humanity was the gap between what states pledged to do and what they actually did. The discrepancy between rhetoric and reality can almost always be explained by politics. Such failings were particularly evident concerning the responsibility to protect. That those seeking to make "never again" more than a slogan require more than moral outrage and shocked consciences is clear from what has *not* happened in Darfur, the DRC, and Zimbabwe, case studies that we explore in some depth in this section.[18] The UN Security Council's dithering since early 2003 in spite of massive murder and displacement in Darfur resembles its inability to address the even longer-running woes of the DRC. Along with mediocre mediation in Zimbabwe, we observe the dramatic disparity between lofty multilateral rhetoric and the collective spinelessness to prevent mass atrocities. In her leaked "end-of-assignment-report," retiring Under-Secretary-General for Oversight Services Inga-Britt Ahlenius asked, "Is there any improvement in general of our capacity to protect the civilians in conflict and distress? ... [W]e seem to be seen less and less as a relevant partner in resolution of world problems."[19] Or, as a group of researchers from the Overseas Development Institute comments, the World Summit resolution "set a high-water mark of rhetorical concern ... but opinion is highly divided on what responsibility this actually implies for international actors."[20]

Darfur

Although conflict has been long-standing between nomadic herders and pastoralists, the ongoing crisis in Darfur dates from early 2003, when rebels from the Sudan Liberation Movement/Army and Justice and Equality Movement (JEM) began attacking government posts in western Sudan. Accusing the Arab-dominated government in Khartoum of neglecting the Darfur region and of oppressing non-Arabs, rebel groups sought to exploit the army's overstretch in southern Sudan, the site of a 30-year conflict between its mostly Christian and animist populations with Muslims in the north.

The government armed and supplied the *janjaweed*—militiamen from primarily nomadic Muslim tribes—to attack Darfur's sedentary ethnic groups. The gruesome numbers are disputed, but estimates are as high as 400,000 dead and 2.7 million displaced. *New York Times* columnist Nicholas Kristof has fought, unsuccessfully, a one-man campaign and laments that "the publishing industry manages to respond more quickly to genocide than the UN and world leaders do."[21] In July 2004, the US Congress condemned Darfur unanimously, voting 422–0 in the House of Representatives with the Senate concurring, that Khartoum was committing genocide.[22] Meanwhile, Secretary of State Colin Powell used the term in Senate testimony in September of that year, perhaps a mistake in that many legalistic hairs are split to determine the applicability of this technical term while the reality of mass atrocities is all too clear.[23]

Roméo Dallaire, the Canadian general in charge of the truly inadequate UN forces during Rwanda's 1994 slaughter, comments: "Having called what is happening in Darfur genocide and having vowed to stop it, it is time for the West to keep its word."[24] In June 2004, the African Union (AU) deployed 60 observers with a force of 300 troops to Darfur as the African Union Mission in the Sudan (AMIS); and the following month, it launched negotiations at the Abuja inter-Sudanese peace talks. While the AU tried to spearhead international political efforts and Khartoum opposed any UN involvement, the Security Council referred Darfur to the ICC in March 2005 and established the UN Mission in the Sudan (UNMIS). This operation's task was to reinforce AMIS and implement the 2005 Comprehensive Peace Agreement ending the even more deadly conflict in southern Sudan. The reluctance to endanger that tenuous peace agreement helps explain the hesitancy by many to press Khartoum over Darfur.

In December 2007, a hybrid United Nations and African Union Mission in Darfur (UNAMID) officially took over from AMIS. *Global Peace Operations 2009* describes the military effort there as "feckless," with only 17,000 poorly equipped troops eventually to be spread out over an area four times the size of France. Meanwhile, Qatar, the UN, the AU, and the Arab League sponsored talks in Doha in February 2009. The Sudanese government and JEM signed the "Agreement of Goodwill and Confidence-Building for the Settlement of the Problem in Darfur." The so-called Doha Peace Process subsequently stalled.

The lack of robust international military efforts has been matched on the legal front. Indeed, the International Criminal Court's involvement in Darfur seemingly has created more problems than it has solved. Half-hearted "intervention," be it military or legal, strengthens the hand of culprits. After issuing an indictment in 2008 without any way to ensure compliance, the ICC then issued an arrest warrant for President Omar Hassan Ahmad al-Bashir in March 2009 on the charge of crimes against humanity and war crimes; and for good measure, it added the charge of genocide in mid-2010. Criticism of the theatrical and self-serving personality of Chief Prosecutor Luis Moreno-Ocampo and of the ICC's being a "white man's court" (because of the large number of African cases on the docket) may or may not be justified,[25] but the counter-productive nature of certain ICC actions has become apparent. Many observers called on the Security Council to exercise its Rome-Statute right to defer prosecution for a year to facilitate the peace process in Darfur as well as to keep intact the tenuous agreements pertaining to the county's long-standing civil war. As a result, the spoilers' hands were strengthened. The Non-Aligned Movement, the Group of 77 developing countries, and regional groups of the global South superficially at least backed al-Bashir, who in turn felt empowered and halted assistance by thirteen foreign and three national NGOs to the almost 3 million internally displaced people in Darfur. Those actions might qualify as yet another crime against humanity.

By the end of 2009—some two and a half years after its authorization—the UNAMID force was about 75 percent operational. But even then, it was overwhelmed and unable to react to atrocities; it ignominiously offers "the specter of a replay of the combined failures in Srebrenica and Rwanda," according to *Global Peace Operations 2009*. Moreover, implementing the responsibility to protect would dictate overriding sovereignty, rather than waiting for an invitation from those in Khartoum who are responsible for atrocities in the first place. Unlike peace operations elsewhere—and also in contrast to Kenya where a reluctant government was dragged along—in Darfur the international force "faces willful opposition from a virulently anti-UNAMID Sudanese government that banks on other states' reluctance to challenge its sovereignty."[26]

Public attention by such groups as the Save Darfur Coalition may have helped to improve somewhat the situation of displaced persons from the height of violence in 2003–5. But international military action has been too little and too late. And, the interesting question is not only whether the infamous moral hazard has exacerbated matters,[27] but also whether the human rights coalition that has now made Darfur a defining call to action will get in the way not only of humanitarian action but also of a political solution. Why might a strong human rights stand be an obstacle to keeping people alive and finding a just solution?

The argument among many humanitarians is as follows. The human rights coalition is intent on turning up the heat on the Khartoum government and thus backs the International Criminal Court's indictments of sitting Sudanese leaders for war crimes. But what is the government's response? To act as if it has nothing to lose and consequently to kick out aid agencies on the grounds that they are part of an international coalition that is more interested in regime change than getting aid to affected populations.

Also, once the human rights coalition charges the Sudanese government with genocide, then negotiations seem like a sell-out. But what is the alternative? What impact will international pressure have on the fragile peace between Khartoum and the autonomous government of southern Sudan? We do not propose any answers, but Sudan has been an illustration of the divide between humanitarian and human rights coalitions and the difficulty of knowing what is the right kind of intervention at what point in an armed conflict. In any event, without robust, committed, and effective international involvement Darfur's suffering will continue.[28]

Democratic Republic of the Congo

Hostilities in the DRC since 1998 are referred to interchangeably as the "Second Congo War," the "Great War of Africa," and even "Africa's World War."[29] The war officially ended in 2003 following the regionally brokered 2002 Global All-Inclusive Accord, which established a transitional government and led to elections in 2005. But fighting—most notably in the eastern provinces of North and South Kivu—continues to claim countless lives amidst atrocities including a continuing war on women. Since 1998, almost 5.5 million people have died while another 5 million have been displaced, and hundreds of thousands of women have been sexually assaulted.[30]

The International Rescue Committee regularly updates these gruesome figures, and already their 2007 mortality survey had awarded the DRC the dubious honor of being the world's most lethal armed conflict since World War II.[31] The vast majority of deaths have resulted from nonviolent, easily-treatable causes such as malaria, diarrhea, pneumonia, and malnutrition that, however, are directly tied to the war and its aftermath. An estimated 45,000 people continue to die every month, and the UN describes the frequency and intensity of rape as the worst in the world.[32] A recent trend in Congo's rape epidemic is the upsurge in the number of male rape victims.[33]

The UN's peacekeeping and electoral efforts in the DRC, its largest ever, appear feeble in comparison with the magnitude of the suffering. In November 1999, the UN authorized the UN Organization Mission in the Democratic Republic of Congo (MONUC) to implement the Lusaka Ceasefire Agreement, which had been signed a few months earlier by the heads of state of Angola, the DRC, Namibia, Rwanda, Uganda, Zambia, and Zimbabwe. Initially deploying a force of 3,900 military observers with a monitoring and humanitarian assistance mandate, MONUC's strength has increased with additional soldiers and police. In 2009, there were more than 18,000 uniformed personnel, still ludicrously inadequate for such a vast territory.[34]

October 2006 elections replaced the transitional government in December with one led by Joseph Kabila, but state fragility made the DRC fertile ground for further conflict fueled and funded by neighbors. Since November 2007 when the governments of the DRC and Rwanda supposedly agreed to refrain from arming belligerents, MONUC has shifted to providing operational support to DRC government forces—the Forces Armées de la République Démocratique du Congo (FARDC)—to implement a program of disarmament, demobilization, and reintegration (DDR).

In early 2008, Kinshasa convened a conference with rebel groups, neighboring countries, MONUC, and other countries. The inability of both the FARDC and MONUC to protect civilians, however, was exposed in 2008 when the Congrès National pour la Défense du Peuple of Laurent Nkunda launched a series of attacks, including a major offensive against the eastern city of Goma, before eventually calling for a unilateral ceasefire.

DDR efforts have failed with "serious consequences for MONUC's public image." UN peacekeepers were allegedly involved in "sexual exploitation, the smuggling of gold, and fraternizing with rebel groups."[35] The allegations were an ugly reminder of the scandal of 2004 when peacekeepers and civilian personnel were guilty of rape, prostitution, and pedophilia.

The presence of foreign armed fighters, including the Forces Démocratiques de Libération du Rwanda, some of whom are alleged to have participated in Rwanda's genocide, remains troubling. *Global Peace Operations 2009* reports that UN performance has "exposed the disconnect between MONUC's mandate and its capabilities" and threatened to undermine UN peacekeeping "as an effective conflict management instrument."[36]

If the numbers alone do not qualify this case as requiring robust R2P attention, the existence of rape and other mass atrocities along with the specific targeting of civilians should. Moreover, the underlying dynamics—the culture of impunity, hate speech, ethnic conflict, enormous economic disparities, and a long history of ugly atrocities—provide unsettling omens. The crimes of the past undoubtedly are ample indicators of likely future atrocities. Yet the size of an effective outside intervention and the requisite political will would be so large that the application of R2P is even less likely than a decade ago. Indeed, the central government in Kinshasa, in the lead-up to the dubious celebration of the results of 50 years of independence in 2010, threatened to reduce the UN force as a means to assert its sovereignty.

Zimbabwe

As head of government since 1980, Robert Mugabe's image as valiant guerrilla hero has been replaced by one of a tyrant refusing to abdicate his throne. He has unleashed violence against political opponents and implemented policies designed to consolidate his personal position that have led to the country's precipitous economic decline since 1998. That year, as head of the South African Development Community's Organ on Politics, Defence, and Security, Mugabe sent troops to the DRC to prop up Laurent Kabila. Jealous of the attention paid to South Africa's iconic Nelson Mandela, Mugabe's attempt was widely viewed as an unsuccessful effort to establish himself as southern Africa's leading statesman.

In 2000, Mugabe began a fast-track land reform and resettlement program to redistribute white-owned farms, mostly to his cronies.

Frenzied and chaotic implementation led to a sharp decline in Zimbabwe's agricultural exports and hard-currency reserves, which has continued unabated since. Mugabe's decision to print hundreds of trillions of Zimbabwean dollars led to hyper-inflation and chronic oil and food shortages. In 2005, the government launched Operation Murambatsvina, an urban demolitions campaign that forcibly displaced hundreds of thousands of people, virtually all supporters of the opposition. Some 3.5 million people fled abroad, and at least 1 million are internally displaced.[37]

Whereas inadequate regional and UN peacekeeping forces were deployed in Darfur and the DRC, international efforts to resolve the crisis in Zimbabwe have consisted merely of ineffective sanctions and even less impressive diplomacy. To repeat what we said above, military, legal, or economic intervention against the wishes of a sovereign state should either be robust or not attempted. Limpid action merely strengthens the resolve of thugs and even permits them to mobilize sympathy via a predictable dynamic of "rally-round-the-flag."

In 2002, the Commonwealth suspended Zimbabwe on charges of human rights abuses committed during the land distribution campaign and of election tampering. In 2002, the European Union imposed targeted sanctions in response to the land reform program, and in 2003 the United States also imposed sanctions. In 2006, the IMF suspended financial and technical assistance. However, China and Russia vetoed comprehensive UN sanctions against Zimbabwe in 2008. The fact that punitive sanctions were championed by the former colonial master, Britain, and by other Western powers made the rhetoric of "imperialism" harder to dismiss in Africa than one might have expected in the face of massive human rights abuses and the bankruptcy—certainly moral if not yet economic—of one of the continent's wealthiest countries that had inherited some of its best infrastructure.

Nonetheless, regional diplomatic efforts were, if possible, even more inept. In particular, Thabo Mbeki (now South Africa's former president) let solidarity with one of the leading father figures of African liberation override any concern for the welfare of Zimbabweans. As chief mediator, he was unwilling to apply South Africa's economic and transport leverage, and this reluctance has not changed since South Africa's current president, Jacob Zuma, took over as the titular leader of African diplomacy.

The results of presidential and parliamentary elections in March 2008 were withheld by the regime for weeks, and Mugabe refused to concede defeat in the presidential election even after acknowledging that Morgan Tsvangirai's Movement for Democratic Change had gained a number of parliamentary seats. Action by the Security Council was impossible as evidenced by the double (Russian and Chinese) veto of sanctions in July 2008. Thabo Mbeki tried once again in September 2008 to broker a power-sharing deal that left Mugabe as president and later installed Tsvangirai as prime minister in February 2009. The hardship caused by food and oil shortages, forced displacement, and political violence has led to a continuing sharp decline in life expectancy among Zimbabweans—in 2006 the World Health Organization ranked the country worst in the world, with 34 years for females and 37 years for males.[38] While it is in a gray legal area in terms of constituting a crime against humanity, in 2008 a cholera epidemic spread throughout Zimbabwe and caused at least 4,000 deaths before spreading into neighboring countries.[39]

The Security Council has been even less active in Zimbabwe than in Darfur and the DRC. Given widespread and self-induced suffering, this record provides yet another illustration of anemic political will, both regional and international, to mitigate mass atrocities. African diplomatic disarray and the differences between the West and South Africa have resulted in a total absence of regional unity and international muscle. This case is a benchmark that suggests how difficult it is to move governments to act against the preferences of other states even when they result in mass atrocities.

If not Zimbabwe, what would qualify as an R2P self-induced atrocity?

What is "new" about the new humanitarianism?

Readers should be aware that more than typical academic caution leads us to proceed gingerly. Although we come down on the side of more change and less continuity in contemporary humanitarian affairs, several reasons explain why that judgment is harder than it appears on the surface, why we equivocate in responding to the query that is the heading for this section.

The first is that there are other historical periods that compare with the current moment—perhaps not in terms of absolute size and scale or of the technological capacity to reach vulnerable populations, but certainly in terms of ambitions and constraints on access. Said otherwise, too many contemporary accounts proceed as if humanitarianism began with the end of the Cold War, thereby demonstrating little historical memory and restricting meaningful comparisons across periods.

For instance, aid workers sometimes talk as if Rwanda were the first time that they confronted militarized camps, which conveniently overlooks uncomfortable experiences in El Salvador, Lebanon, Cambodia, and Pakistan in the 1970s and 1980s. Those suggesting that the dangers of being too closely identified with a warring faction started with Somalia in the early 1990s overlook the controversial positions taken by aid agencies in places like Vietnam, Biafra, and Nicaragua during the Cold War. Those hinting that only in the last two decades have aid agencies had to ponder the value of neutrality and independence conveniently ignore the extent to which such debates accompanied the Holocaust, the Vietnamese intervention in Cambodia in 1978, and pervasive crises in Ethiopia since the late 1960s.

Our second qualification, to which we alluded in Chapter 1, results from the fundamental absence of longitudinal data on such basic categories as expenditure, income, number of organizations, and overall activities. The struggle to assemble common stylized facts complicates generalizations not only because the numbers themselves are dodgy but also because they can be, and have been, manipulated for political purposes and fund-raising, thereby further complicating the interpretation of any so-called hard data. Moreover, it seems likely but not certain that better data alone could account for at least some of the reported growth. The combination of these factors presents a challenge to embed sufficiently the present moment in historical perspective—as does the need for harder numbers and comparative analysis.

A final and slightly more academic nitpicking word is in order. The adjective "new" does not indicate that wars have only begun recently but rather that the customary dynamics from the two previous historical periods have changed substantially enough to merit this adjective. While it is commonly assumed that there has been an upswing in the number, intensity, and duration of civil wars since 1989, data indicate that the overall quantity of conflicts throughout the 1990s actually decreased while negotiated settlements increased.[40] Both states and nonstate actors have always manipulated war victims.[41] Washington and Moscow selectively supported "their" refugees engaged in the fights against communism and capitalism, respectively, and guerrillas (sometimes in the war theater and sometimes in exile) and refugee groups were able to get support from their proxy patrons using the same logic.

Hence, we believe that "changed" is a preferable label for armed conflicts in the historical period since 1989 and for the various humanitarianisms that have resulted. In his *Taming the Sovereigns*, Kal Holsti offers a way to understand these labels, by integrating factors and providing the context for historical developments. His subtitle, *Institutional Change in International Politics*, identifies reasons why the kinds of wars experienced since 1989 might well be considered "new." He notes that "a narrow conception of change fails to acknowledge the importance of other *sources* of change (such as ideas and revolutions), other *types* of change (such as the growth of nonstate actors and international civil society), and other *consequences* of change (such as global governance)."[42]

Our view thus is not so much that entirely new elements have appeared as that elements once thought dormant or extinct, tangential, or even irrelevant have come back to the fore and been combined in ways that were heretofore unremarkable or unknown. Hence, changes in war since 1989 are quantitatively and qualitatively significant and combined in such previously unfamiliar ways that we can understand why some observers of the current generation of wars call them "new." More significantly the amount of energy devoted to doing something about them has incresed, unleashing novel dynamics.

As a result, the traditional standard operating procedures of humanitarians are no longer unquestioned; they are hotly contested. We trust that by now readers have understood why we chose the title of this volume.

Conclusion: unlimited ambitions—and whose?

Is there anything new in humanitarianism? For us, the answer lies in its growing ambitions, bordering at times on hubris. President Woodrow Wilson has been lampooned for declaring World War I as the war to end all wars; and many aid agencies can be similarly mocked for believing that they can eliminate the root causes of injustice or end global poverty. Whether we choose to deal harshly or sympathetically with such statements, there is no question that humanitarianism has become more brash, bold, and grandly ambitious than ever before. How do we account for this state of affairs?

There is the possibility that states and deeper structural imperatives made humanitarians enlarge the scope of their activities beyond the provision of immediate assistance to victims of war and of natural disasters. Aid-worker-turned-academic Mark Duffield argues that broader discourses of security, liberalism, and development have shaped what humanitarianism is and what it does—in other words, it is implicated in a broader set of global discourses. Such thoughts do not have to lead to the sort of conspiracy-theory arguments best associated with Noam Chomsky—in which humanitarianism is nothing more than an instrument of imperial design—though they often do. Our view is that we can certainly appreciate the global forces that are shaping humanitarianism's character without succumbing to a simple-minded view that humanitarianism is nothing more than the fumes of power.

There are many reasons why aid agencies would want to expand. Some reasons are sincere and well-intentioned; some are not. It is difficult to look on the suffering of others and not want to do something, especially if one's vocation is already bound up with an ethics of care. And in a world in which humanity and impartiality are signature principles of action, it is indefensible to attend to the pain of one population while ignoring the pain of another. After a while it becomes unbearably disheartening to be continually saving lives without imagining how to tackle the root causes of suffering and justice. Why keep applying band-aids when more invasive treatment is necessary and may be available? If the goal is to truly relieve suffering by eliminating it, then it is difficult to feel gratified by providing temporary relief; instead, humanitarians understandably will desire to address the very conditions that produce a demand for their services.

Another factor potentially influencing this expansion is psychological, deriving from the personal strain of providing relief in war zones. Aid workers migrate from one nightmare to another, comforted only by the fact that, at best, they provide temporary respite. This sort of existence takes a high emotional toll. Relief workers live in a twilight zone of hopelessness, believing that their just acts cannot begin to change the circumstances that give cause for their services. Wanting to believe that they actually are helping to build a better world, they began to treat human rights, conflict resolution, and nation-building as extensions of humanitarianism.[43]

For instance, before the 1980s the UNHCR leaped into action only after populations crossed an international border. Yet many UNHCR staff bristled at this restriction, wanting to take on a more pro-active role. Their wish came true in the 1980s, as the UNHCR began trying to prevent refugee flows, to get at their "root causes," and to lobby for "state responsibility."[44] From there it was a small step for the UNHCR to become involved in eliminating the causes underlying the need to flee and ensuring that repatriated refugees stayed at home; next it began promoting human rights, the rule of law, and development. Ethics of care and discourses of impartiality can cause well-meaning people to want to do more and more. Indeed, humanitarianism's slope is quintessentially slippery.

Whatever one's judgment about the nature of humanitarian action after 9/11 as well as before, the forces of destruction, production, and salvation combine in various ways in distinct historical periods to help define the meaning, scope, and scale of humanitarianism. Although their relative weights shift within the three periods discussed in this book and are experienced differently in different parts of the globe, three generalizations emerge from the humanitarian debris strewn across the historical periods. One, humanitarianism is constantly being reshaped by the world in which it tries to mitigate suffering; and any attempt to assess the present should have as a point of departure a clear- rather than misty-eyed view of a complicated past. Two, different strands of humanitarianism have different relationships to the forces of destruction, production, and salvation; and because of such relationships, the impact will be felt differentially by aid agencies. Three, the meaning of humanitarianism has expanded: human rights, development, democracy promotion, and peace-building were once considered distinctive fields of social life but increasingly are bundled together in a general ethic of moral caretaking under the humanitarian banner.

In short, humanitarianism has become institutionalized, internationalized, and prominent on the global agenda; and it is used to justify, legitimate, and galvanize action. But a continuing feature is that it is contested. What about the future?

6 Humanitarianism's past and possible futures
Ten guiding questions

Humanitarianism is here to stay and will continue to grow and evolve through good times and bad, but what kind exactly will evolve? What varieties do we want to see in the world? As should be clear by now, humanitarianism is a work in progress, at times it has been worked over by the world and at times a work designed by humanitarians themselves. Although we cannot predict how humanitarianism will develop in the coming decades, we can use the past to alert us to a range of possibilities. This chapter does not offer empirical predictions. Instead, it highlights the normative issues that have and will continue to confront the humanitarian sector.

Several caveats should be specified. The ten questions posed here do not exhaust the ethical dilemmas and tough moral choices that those in the sector confront daily; rather, we have selected those that best tease out identity-defining issues. Also, there is a stark difference between the ideal and the possible. Humanitarianism exists because we live on a planet that is filled with injustice, violence, and suffering. Aid workers try to make that world a little less horrible, but they do so with too few resources while working with and relying upon many who benefit from the world as it currently exists. So, they must compromise, and the best that they can hope is to avoid making rotten comprises. Lastly, there are no crystal clear answers to the questions posed. Indeed, we do not even agree about the kind of humanitarianism that we would both like to see or the shape of acceptable compromises.

Question #1: What should humanitarianism do?

We live in a world of multiple humanitarianisms, not a single humanitarianism. While aid workers unite and divide over many issues, perhaps the most important is the overall purpose of their common enterprise. They agree that their work reflects the desire to relieve the suffering of strangers, but they have very different ideas about how involved they should become in the lives of others. As we saw, some tackle symptoms and aspire to save lives in immediate peril. Best known among such organizations is the International Committee of the Red Cross, but there are many others whose bottom line is the number of lives saved. Another camp believes that it is not enough to save those in danger but must also address in the short- and long-term causes of suffering. For those organizations, humanitarianism is about altering the underlying patterns of power, inequality, and injustice that are supposedly responsible for limiting the opportunities of peoples and exposing them to harm in the first place.

Should humanitarianism limit itself to saving lives at immediate risk or be more ambitious? Each side has its talking points. Emergency relief acknowledges that coming to the rescue is not ambitious, but it is a well-defined goal that can be accomplished. Conversely, if humanitarians set out to tackle the causes, not only do they frequently not know what to do but they also find access to affected populations limited as a result. Those in power hardly welcome aid agencies that want to change the world. The perfect thus should not be the enemy of the good. The more that humanitarianism cozies up to the powers that be, the more that it sacrifices neutrality and independence. All these actions and compromises have another consequence because they are viewed as political: in war zones humanitarians will find themselves turned into enemy combatants.

Those who are more ambitious argue that humanitarianism exists in a political world and makes compromises with politics, and thus that there are ways in which politics can be its friend. What is the moral defense for saving a life today if that person dies in a few months from starvation and without a living wage or access to bare necessities? If the US government is ready to commit its military power to try and liberate Afghans, and especially women and girls, from the stranglehold of the Taliban and Al Qaeda, why not recognize that military might and humanitarianism may be on the same side (though for different reasons)? Why not adjust relief and development activities on the ground so that they help Americans win "hearts and minds"?

Although these questions and dilemmas are generally directed at specific situations, they also relate to broader considerations about global justice. Should humanitarianism reform or revolutionize the world? The ICRC and fellow travelers do not attempt to transform the world but merely make it a little less horrible. The ICRC has never been anti-war or espoused pacifism. It does not endeavor to eliminate war but rather ensure that combatants abide by certain rules that make armed conflict somewhat less barbaric if not more civilized.

Some accuse the ICRC of selling out because reform means little more than maintaining the status quo. In response, the ICRC and other symptom-treating organizations argue that they have nothing against those who want to change the world, but in the meantime someone has to be attentive to the here and now. Yet the ICRC and other like-minded organizations are perhaps too modest. Lurking behind their seemingly reformist impulses, at times, beats the heart of a radical. Even those who engage in emergency relief aspire to practice a kind of politics that protests the idea that our obligations are limited by arbitrary political borders. They practice a politics of humanity, of cosmopolitanism, that challenges a world organized around the idea that sovereign states should monopolize our duties. And they certainly espouse a radical idea—at least for card-carrying members of the Realist fan club—that sovereignty does not include a license to murder. And they spend a fair bit of time trying to change how states, militaries, militias, and even corporations understand their responsibilities; in doing so, they are not only trying to change behavior but also how individuals and institutions see themselves in relationship to the vulnerable.

Those aid organizations that aspire to tackle the structures of inequality and injustice often have in mind a radical restructuring of domestic and global society. Certainly an important role exists for those organizations that are focused on providing relief, but they also have an obligation not only to future generations but also to the victims of oppression and violence to try and provide the kind of protection that comes from living in a more just society.

Although such statements sound good, the devil is in the details. What exactly is a radical humanitarian vision for a just society? In many cases those who come bearing models of utopias assume that their particular ones are universal but overlook cultural biases. In the nineteenth century, for instance, the missionary was famously convinced that Christ was the answer whereas many of today's humanitarians place their faith in economic opportunities, the rule of law, and democracy. Those who come bearing markets, human rights, and elections might be right that liberalism is the answer; and it is equally possible that nineteenth-century missionaries were right about the teachings of Christ.

But there are two immediate problems. First, the new humanitarians often are trying to force others to be free, a proposition from Jean-Jacques Rousseau that can have disastrous consequences, as the immediate aftermath of the French Revolution of 1789 illustrates. Radical overhaul from above not only lacks legitimacy but also can justify and rationalize unspeakable forms of violence and coercion. Second, those who are certain about where others should go might not be so certain about how to get there. Chasing pots of gold at the end of rainbows might lead to years wandering in the wilderness. We know very little about how to build legitimate states after war, how the promotion of democracy, markets, and human rights intersect, and so on. No wonder that there are as many strategies as plans. In short, those seeking to eliminate the root causes of injustice and violence may have more passion than know-how which is almost always worrisome.

Question #2: What can humanitarianism accomplish?

There is an obvious connection between the kind of humanitarianism that we want and what we believe it can actually do. Part of the reason behind a limited and cautious humanitarianism is the presumption that we know how to treat symptoms whereas we do not have a clue how to eliminate the causes of violence. Although we agree with Elvis Costello that there is nothing funny about wanting "peace, love, and under-standing," it is easy to sound like a contestant for a beauty pageant if we say it too often and with too much earnestness. Striving to make the world a better place certainly is not a bad idea, but if our humanitarianism is fixated on creating peace on the earth then probably a lot of people will die from neglect as a result.

Yet a too limited version of humanitarianism may very well down-grade what is possible. It is not as if we are as ignorant today as we were several decades ago regarding what may be done to improve the lives of vulnerable populations in marginal situations and emerging from violence. There have been advances that make it reasonable to try and find a middle ground between practicing emergency medicine and witchcraft. There is greater attention to evaluating effectiveness. There is greater attention to learning lessons. There is greater attention to appreciating the unintended effects of good intentions. There is greater attention to integrating system-wide effects and linkages between areas once treated as separate and independent.

There are no magic bullets—which we should recall whenever someone proposes the mother of all solutions whether it is in the form of micro-finance, an increase in foreign aid, or even the elimination of humanitar-ianism. If we examine both different sectors (say, security and health) and policies (say, reintegration of child soldiers, how to protect women in refugee camps, and malaria prevention), we find that a lot more is known today than even a decade ago. And, if we look a little more closely at broad trends, we see great strides over the last several decades, includ-ing silent successes like an impressive reduction in the rate of maternal deaths during childbirth and more educational opportunities for girls.

Aiming low might help protect us from the invariable disappointment that occurs from falling short of grand goals, but there are some potentially powerful possibilities on the horizon if we gaze long and hard enough.

Question #3: Which principles, when?

Although many portray the principles of humanitarian action as if they were etched on stone tablets brought down from Mount Sinai, in fact they are products of history, ethical imagination, and practical considerations. In certain respects nearly all of the principles of humanitarianism—which, it bears repeating, were not codified by the ICRC as humanitarianism's principles until the 1960s—arose because they were functional for engaging in rescue and relief in highly charged political circumstances. These principles, in other words, are human inventions and represent solutions to the problem of securing access to those in need in concrete cases.

Many argue that the principles of humanity and impartiality are universal, but it is probably more accurate to say that it is their presumed universality that gives them their moral power. Moreover, aid workers have a vested interest in enforcing this interpretation because it greases the gears of humanitarian action. There is agreement that the principles of neutrality and independence are more instrumental than intrinsic, but disagreement about whether humanitarians are obligated to follow them is dependent on the circumstances on the ground. Some actors, namely the ICRC, argue that these principles are part of the humanitarian identity while others insist that they are functional under some circumstances but downright dysfunctional under others. The ICRC is now nearly alone in religiously applying them in many theaters because for many other aid workers the principles are derived from the situation on the ground (and often affected by the sheer emotion of the situation). We do know one thing, though: the question of which principles when will not be settled in the near future, if ever.

Independence means that an aid agency is not associated with anyone who might have a vested interest in the conflict. Toward that end, agencies have constructed all kinds of different rules for themselves: how much money they can take from governments; which governments have clean and which dirty money; whether they can be seen speaking in public to government officials or representatives from militaries; how far their sleeping quarters should be from government ministries and other aid agencies that are seen as having been co-opted by one side or another; and whether it is even acceptable to catch a ride or share a meal with someone who is not completely pure.

There are sensible reasons why aid agencies have developed these guidelines, but who are they for? Many insist that following them helps convince those on the ground that aid workers are truly independent, which thus helps create humanitarian space with access to those in need. However, many recent surveys suggest that these rules are often lost on recipients. Specifically, for many local communities, foreigners are foreigners. And while sometimes distinctions are made between good and bad varieties, by and large anyone who shows up is guilty until proven innocent. Consequently, many of these rituals of independence appear to leave a greater impression on other aid organizations and funding agencies than they do on recipients.

Debates about the purposes and principles of humanitarianism, as we have seen, are also related to differing views regarding the relationship between humanitarianism and politics: whereas some argue that humanitarianism should avoid politics at all costs, others insist that there is an unacceptable cost to avoiding politics. There are strong arguments on both sides. It is the perception that aid workers exist outside of politics and in the realm of ethics that allows them to get access to those in need; there can be little doubt that the more humanitarian action is associated with one side in a conflict or power struggle, the more difficult it is to establish a safe presence on the ground. Yet the argument against this position is that humanitarianism becomes a cloak, hiding the existence of politics when politics is all around.

Even the most dogmatically apolitical aid workers are deeply involved in politics, whether it is a politics of resistance to a world of incredible suffering or a politics that tries to minimize unnecessary suffering during armed conflicts. Does this mean that humanitarians should simply embrace their inner politician? In recent years this position has grown in popularity in word and deed. Although there is something to be said for truth in advertising, there also is a danger in advertising and promising too much—perhaps to the point of discrediting and endangering a more modest humanitarianism.

Question #4: Do we want a militarized humanitarianism?

The debates over purposes, principles, and politics are especially sensitive when it comes to the relationship between humanitarianism and the military. For the most part, humanitarians want little to do with militaries, militias, and those toting weapons. The dangers are obvious: the moment that humanitarians associate with militaries and other armed groups is the instant that their independence and moral authority are stained. At the same time, nearly all aid agencies recognize the requirement for close cooperation with if not active assistance from the military.[1] Even the ICRC depends on the permission of military authorities to do their work.

Additionally, militaries are used to moving lots of equipment and supplies over long distances in short periods of time, which is often precisely what is needed during an emergency situation. If they are offering, why not accept a ride? And what happens when aid agencies encounter outright violent resistance to their efforts to provide life-saving relief? Or when local militias and militaries demand too much of a cut (or more euphemistically a "tax") of a relief convoy, thus not only depriving those in desperate need of additional succor but also fueling the very armed groups that are engaged in combat operations and benefiting from the misery of others? Is there not a role for some kind of armed convoy? In Somalia even the ICRC experimented with "technicals" (armed local protection agents), and the United Nations and some NGOs make use of private military companies.

In any case, it was an innovation to create physical—instead of merely legal or metaphorical—space for humanitarians in which relief could be administered because military forces were present. Shannon Beebe and Mary Kaldor observe that since the turbulent 1990s, "the distinction between 'battle space' and 'humanitarian space' was dissolving."[2] In 2000 US secretary of state Condoleezza Rice famously argued, "We don't need to have the 82nd Airborne escorting kids to kindergarten,"[3] but experience suggests that perhaps she was wrong.

While not entirely, and in some instances not remotely, effective in creating secure space, the use of the military in humanitarian crises represents the grandest ambitions of the international humanitarian system.[4] Building on the example of the "corridors of tranquility" in Sudan, other examples of safe spaces established in the 1990s include: "safe havens" in northern Iraq (1991–2003); "safe areas" in Bosnia and Herzegovina (1993–95); and "secure humanitarian areas" in Rwanda (French Opération Turquoise, 1994).[5] These were also related to similar robust military efforts with substantial humanitarian dimensions in Somalia, Haiti, Kosovo, Albania, and East Timor.

No development over the last two decades has produced more consternation and wildly differing perspectives among humanitarians than deploying what the International Commission on Intervention and State Sovereignty called "the use of military force for human protection purposes."[6] And to state the obvious, when an international decision— sometimes by the UN Security Council (e.g., in Somalia, Haiti, or Bosnia), or by a regional organization (e.g., by NATO in Kosovo or the Economic Community of West African States in Liberia), or by a coalition of the willing (e.g., in Iraq)—leads to the deployment of war-fighters rather than peacekeepers, the costs and benefits of using over-whelming force are highly controversial. Some (including one of the authors[7]) have pointed to more good than harm in many cases, while others like David Rieff have railed vehemently against military huma-nitarianism and what Michael Ignatieff and other activists have called "a revolution of moral concern."[8] But Rieff believes that militarized humanitarianism has eroded traditional principles and not "actually kept a single jackboot out of a single human face."[9]

These concerns echo George Orwell's passage in *1984*: "If you want a picture of the future, imagine a boot stamping on a human face—forever."[10] Militarized humanitarianism might have a corrupting effect, with actions and compromises that corrode core values. For example in Kosovo,[11] numerous aid agencies were so intent on rescuing Kosovar Albanians from Serbian forces that they subordinated themselves to NATO, downplaying civilian casualties in Serbia and the principle of need-based aid for the Serbian minority in Kosovo.

Question #5: What kind of ethics?

We often speak of a humanitarian ethic, by which we mean the visceral impulse to help suffering strangers. To be a humanitarian is to respond to the suffering of others regardless of their identity, to act selflessly, and to place humanity above other considerations. Stated otherwise, it rebels against a world of self-interest and brute power with its daily bill-of-fare of greed and bloodshed. In fact, multiple ethics run through humanitarian action, and not all of them are necessarily compatible.

Two principal modes of ethical reasoning dominate the theory and practice of humanitarianism: duty-based and consequentialist.[12] Duty-based, otherwise known as deontological, ethics are generally traced back to the philosophy of Immanuel Kant, who argued that some actions are simply good in and of themselves regardless of their consequences. Ethical action, therefore, consists of identifying these intrinsically good actions and then performing one's moral duty. Where does such a moral duty originate? In a word, "humanity," which we respect as an end in itself. And such ends are linked to the idea that we have obligations to help others, within limits, achieve their goals. Humanitarian actors fre-quently articulate some sort of Kantian or duty-based imperative that they must act because of essential obligations that exist as a by-product of their collective humanity. Ethical action, in short, is defined by the act itself. For many the humanitarian ethic means doing one's duty, and that duty requires being willing to help those in need.

Yet many aid workers—in fact, in increasing numbers—espouse a second position, consequentialist ethics, or the rightness of an action is determined by whether it helps to bring about a better outcome than its alternatives. We are morally obligated, therefore, to act in a way that produces the best consequences given the alternatives. The consequentialist position is perhaps most famously associated with Mary Anderson's evocation of the Hippocratic Oath, do no harm.[13] Since then many others have accepted the basic point but have argued that it is impossible to do no harm—all actions have intended and unintended consequences, and the goal is to try and minimize the harm and ensure that the benefits outweigh any negative effects.

Trying to determine the consequences of an act, not only with the luxury of hindsight but also during the fog of war and relief, is incredibly difficult and nearly always imprecise. A pressing question is, "Whose consequences matter?" Frequently calculations refer to some anonymous public; but, in fact, the benefits and consequences are always unevenly distributed, and one person's advantage can be another person's disadvantage. Such matters are particularly evident when trying to determine the balance between order and justice, and whether the former should come at the expense of the latter and who should decide. In addition, there is always the difficulty of determining when we should measure the consequences. It is tempting to issue quarterly reports, but doing so can not only overlook the big picture but also focus everyone on short-term over long-term gains. There also is the question of who evaluates the consequences. Should the UN decide? NGOs on the ground? Local elites? Marginalized groups? In short, the insistence that aid should do more harm than good sounds appealing; but without specifics, it also sounds trite.[14]

In any event, many humanitarian agencies, sometimes at the insistence of their donors, increasingly attempt to gauge the effects of their policies and projects. As they are discovering, though, it is quite difficult to develop and use assessment tools, especially during times of war. If the numbers do not necessarily add up, how can calculations be meaningful, and how can humanitarians determine whether their actions, in the end, are ethical? "'Moral calculus' is not a highly developed form of mathematics," write Marc Lindenberg and Coralie Bryant. "It is hard to know whether one hundred lives saved is worth the price of having inadvertently helped to prolong a conflict by a month. It is even hard to document the numbers of lives lost and saved in such situations."[15] The focus of the 2003 annual report from the Red Cross Movement was precisely about this topic: "The tensions between promoting peace and saving lives, and between order and justice, are not the only clashes of moral goods involving the humanitarian ethic. An equally common problem arises when it seems impossible to realize two rights simultaneously without compromising one of them."[16] Ours is a world in which aid workers often must make choices among a host of ethical goods and bads with insufficient information, and they must do so quickly and somehow be comfortable with acting without confidence that they are choosing correctly.

The tensions between ethical positions are captured in a fascinating conversation between Paul Farmer and his biographer, Tracy Kidder. Farmer's NGO, Partners in Health, went to nearly heroic lengths and spent $20,000 to try and save a child from a rare disease by evacuating him from the hills of Haiti to Boston's Massachusetts General Hospital— where he died a few days later. Expressing his and others' reservations, Kidder wondered whether staff time and money might have been allocated differently and possibly saved hundreds of lives. Farmer responds by attacking the underlying moral terrain of consequences-driven ethics—costs and benefits that largely pivot on the claim that money is more important than lives. So, he proceeds, why are we not discussing the failure of the airline to waive the costs of the flight or the ability of doctors to command such high fees for their services? He rejects the very basis of consequentialist ethics, arguing that, in essence, the moment that he plays God and decides to determine who can live and who can die, he no longer sides with the "losers" but rather is fundamentally one of the "winners" of global order.[17]

Question #6: Is bigger better?

The humanitarian sector has grown dramatically over the last several decades, which means that it can do more and more quickly. Not only are there more and more agencies, foundations, states, and international organizations engaged in some form of humanitarian action, but some private agencies have gone from operating out of a small office in the back of a church or in someone's basement to becoming multinational, business-like organizations. In the early 1980s, for instance, Hany al-Banna started Islamic Relief with little more than a pocketful of pictures of the famine that he showed to relatives and friends to get them to donate; today it is the largest Western-based Islamic agency. World Vision International started in the early 1950s with just a few desks and filing cabinets but today is the largest aid agency in the world with a budget that rivals the foreign assistance operations of many medium-sized countries. As significantly, aid agencies are also engaged in more activities than ever before. Most organizations used to be "multi-mandate" to the extent that they always did emergency relief and something else. But now most organizations are really "multi" and tackling everything from post-traumatic counseling to gender empowerment, from community peace-building to livelihoods.

The heads of transnational corporations insist that being bigger has its advantages for delivering a better product at a more attractive price. So too many leaders of large transnational aid agencies insist that being bigger means that they can do more things more economically, which translates directly into more lives saved. Yet there are various kinds of maladies associated with concentration and centralization in the aid sector, including less room for innovation. As we have seen in other industries, as firms grow they can increase their economies of scale and deliver a better product more cheaply; yet there also is less pressure to innovate, adopt new technologies, search for new cost-saving devices, and improve products. Indeed, growth can become an end in itself, leading to increased benefits to individual staff members with no necessary correlation to either enhanced benefits for clients or stockholders.

The same may be true of the humanitarian sector. After all, roughly seven transnational NGOs constitute an oligopoly. And while we assume that their motives are purer than businesses in the auto and oil industries, humanitarians nevertheless have incentives to keep out new entrants and stop innovating. Anti-trust legislation is not the answer. However, a very real question revolves around the sources and motives for innovation. It is worth pondering whether smaller, if not small, may be beautiful.

Aid agencies do not get bigger by accident—it takes money, and lots of it. An important and increasingly prominent part of the humanitarian sector is fund-raising. Like for-profit corporations, non-profit aid agencies worry constantly about the bottom line. Like modern-day politicians, they are running a permanent campaign and spend as much time thinking about raising money as they do doing good acts. Most aid agencies have no choice but to be highly attentive to fund-raising and cultivating their donors. The key question, of course, is, do they worry to the point that it alters what they do? We honestly do not know. However, our friends in humanitarian organizations spend enough time worrying about the corrupting effects of scrambling for funds that only the most naïve could ignore the possible negative impact.

Question #7: Is it possible to be too professional?

Humanitarianism has grown so much over recent decades that even its vaunted principle of volunteerism has come under pressure to the point that it might not exist. Volunteerism connoted someone with a good heart who was doing it for the love of helping others and not for money or any ulterior goal. Because the wealthy had the luxury, time, and resources, the early days of humanitarianism were dominated by the rich and, in many cases, women who married well or were of independent means. Volunteerism also meant something else: no specialized training was required. Although many humanitarians came from established professional fields such as medicine and social work, by and large anyone could show up who wanted to; in fact, the underlying goal of creating a more cosmopolitan world demanded an open-borders policy and a willingness to embrace all and any comers.

This spirit of volunteerism began to change for several reasons. Volunteerism began to whither once humanitarianism went big time, with established and well-resourced organizations that were constantly patrolling the world and ready and able on short notice to mobilize resources and expertise. Over time, humanitarianism became a sector or a profession (that is, identified with high personal standards in a particular working context), which is not, at least in modern society, run by volunteers.

Second, aid agencies are increasingly operated by staff who depend on this work for their own income. In the past, volunteers typically learned on the job, came in and out when they wanted, and did not necessarily suffer when they made mistakes. In other words, volunteers began as amateurs. But increasingly the humanitarian enterprise frowned upon such naïfs and began demanding that staff have real expertise and rewarded them accordingly. A CEO or CFO of a major not-for-profit aid agency should not require less training or fewer skills or less relevant experience than a CEO or CFO of a for-profit Fortune 500 company. And if they are experts, they expect to be paid accordingly. In the past some poorly paid aid workers stayed in the field for their entire lives, but others treated field work as something for the young and then found another, more stable career when they hit middle-age. Over time many began wanting to pursue a more predictable career pattern and move up the ladder within an organization or switch to a better opportunity in the same sector. In general, staff treat humanitarianism as their career and expect to be paid and have the kinds of employment benefits associated with other occupations.

In this respect, in the late 1980s and early 1990s the humanitarian profession witnessed the same type of development that took place in eighteenth-century Europe when medicine and science became large and prominent enough to justify building their professions. Professionals are expected to have specialized knowledge. In keeping with this expectation, over recent decades the humanitarian sector has increasingly emphasized the importance of earning advanced degrees in such areas as the health sciences and engineering, creating established manuals that can be passed around, and having specialized training programs. Although there is general agreement that professionals draw from a body of knowledge, so far the humanitarian sector has developed it in piecemeal and patchwork fashion, with universities and think tanks establishing their own degrees, courses, and programs that do not necessarily correspond with any agreed coverage. Unlike, say, fields of accounting or nursing, there is as yet little agreement on the canon for humanitarian professionals—what they are expected to know.

Relatedly, failures in the field and bad press have caused aid agencies to try and create a genuine profession. A number of efforts—including a code of conduct for individuals[18] and such efforts as the Sphere Project (a code of conduct of sorts) and ALNAP (or Active Learning Network on Accountability and Performance in Humanitarian Action that pooled evaluation experience)[19]—indicated that humanitarianism is coming of age. As the co-chairs (one a practitioner, one an academic) of Enhancing Learning and Research for Humanitarian Assistance put it, "given the high levels of professionalism that humanitarian workers demand of themselves and each other and, given the increasing investment in capacity building and standard setting across the sector, is the time now right to create an internationally recognised humanitarian profession?"[20] In a survey of some 1,500 aid workers between October 2009 and March 2010, more than 90 percent expressed a strong desire to see professionalism become a vibrant reality.

Various anticipated benefits would follow from the steady march toward the professionalization of humanitarianism. The establishment of "a unified system of professional development, accreditation, and association…could increase accountability, raise the quality and consistency of humanitarian service, open up the profession to talented new recruits, and raise the status of the humanitarian service provider to a level on par with other professional groups," argue Peter Walker and Catherine Ross, the authors of a major scoping study of these developments. "This would support the infrastructure for career paths with lifelong learning opportunities and support the retention of humanitarian workers over decades to come. This also prepares for the forecasted increase in natural and complex disasters where large swathes of civil society in many countries will necessarily be involved in relief work."[21] In short, professionalization would help create a body of knowledge, identifying what professionals need to know and how they should act. In this way, it would also help remove it from politics.

This sounds good, but major problems and concerns remain. One is the difference in perspectives and expectations as an older generation passes the baton to a newer generation of aid workers. Stephen Hopgood's in-depth look into Amnesty International finds a clash when the older volunteer generation encounters a younger, more professional one. The former, "keepers of the flame tend to be deontologists; reformers tend to be consequentialists."[22] Moreover, professionals can become technocrats who are notorious for placing rules above people. Will humanitarianism become so technocratic that it drives out human dimensions from job descriptions? Another is whether professionalization will open or close the door to qualified newcomers. Professionals need degrees and certificates, which, in turn, require money, which, in turn, are unevenly distributed. In other words, will professionalization make it more or less difficult to recruit new talent, especially among the less privileged and in the Third World? Who decides what body of knowledge is relevant? What happens to the spirit of volunteerism, which is closely associated with the desire to encourage people to think of themselves as, and act as if they are, part of a common humanity?

One of the real attractions of humanitarianism is that it welcomes all comers and anticipates that those who give will be changed as much, if not more, than those who receive. Will the move from volunteerism to professionalism eliminate a genuinely cosmopolitan spirit? In the aftermath of the devastating earthquake in Haiti in January 2010, for instance, many vociferously objected to John Travolta's piloting supplies for the Church of Scientology and church members taking Haitian children abroad for adoption. But in many respects, as Hopgood provocatively argues, such efforts represented the best of the humanitarian spirit in action.[23]

Question #8: Can we mobilize action without creating a world of "victims"?

Suffering often leads to compassionate action, but we tend to be moved not by the mere presence of suffering. Instead, we are instigated to act by the needless suffering of innocents and victims, who are too weak, powerless, or vulnerable to help themselves. Accordingly, while there is a surfeit of suffering in the world, only some of it inspires action. What seems an especially powerful stimulus is the suffering of innocent women and children, of vulnerable civilians of all types trapped in armed conflicts, of those viewed as disposable and even sacrificial.

Yet, like everything else humanitarian, mobilizing action on behalf of the innocent is not as straightforward and ethically pure as it might seem at first glance; two related issues demand our attention. First, before acting we must be cognizant of victims around the world, but this may require some degree of exploitation of the very people we want to help.

Who is responsible for alerting us to the suffering of others? States and intergovernmental organizations especially of the UN system have certainly demonstrated the capacity to bring attention to the plight of vulnerable populations. However, when they do such work we view them as having a political agenda of one sort or another, and so we typically discount their claims in favor of those who are viewed as apolitical and beyond reproach—namely, nongovernmental organizations. No one should be so naïve as to believe that NGOs are free from politics, but they normally get the benefit of the doubt because of the presumption that they are speaking on behalf of the powerless and in defense of universal values. In today's world NGOs are, more often than not, responsible for bringing attention to emergencies and advertising what MSF calls the forgotten or silent crises.

How do they do it? The first international humanitarian campaign, the abolitionist movement that we encountered in Chapter 2, operated without the benefit of visual imagery. Since the invention of the camera, however, images (at first photographs and later film and video) have been as essential to NGOs as energy bars and field hospitals. But images are more than just pictures out of context; NGOs and others spend considerable energy trying to embed these images within a storyline or narrative. Images, even more so than facts, never speak for themselves. NGOs and others spend a great deal of time providing narratives that invest these images with emotion and compassion. The humanitarian sector lives the adage of "one picture is worth a thousand words." In fact, one good picture probably can be worth hundreds of thousands of dollars in donations.

As a general rule, the more graphic the image and the more it screams "innocent victim," the more effective it will be in mobilizing compassion, action, and money. Typically we do not give to happy children; instead we give to those with bloated bellies and flies swarming around their sores and eyelids, who are separated from their parents and their communities. Typically we do not give to women who appear strong and confident; instead we give to women who appear to be victims of their circumstances and their culture. Typically most of the images do not include men, or at least not vigorous men between the ages of 16 and 50. We need horror stories, footage preceded by warnings that we are about to see something graphic and disturbing. Obscenity works—mobilizing action depends on the exploitation of the suffering of others. We need to capture people at their most raw and vulnerable, least flattering, and most emotionally exposed moments.

Aid agencies are drawn instinctively to disaster pornography; they are only giving the compassionate what they want.

But at what cost? Those who object to such images argue that being exploitative of other people's circumstances is never proper or ethically correct. Just because it works does not make it right. But what if the victims give consent? What if they are willing to be "exploited" in order to get the story out and bring more attention to their plight? If they are, then is it more acceptable exploitation? Are there limits on what we should be allowed to show? We might concede that images of some suffering are acceptable, but that "snuff films" are not. Who decides? If there is no agreed limit, are we likely to see a spiral in which aid agencies use increasingly graphic images to compete with each other for donations? And what are the effects of these images on the viewer? We hope that they will bring out the best in people, but they might also bring out the worst.

For decades humanitarians have worried that such images contribute to demeaning victims, to perceptions of difference about the "other." Some viewers may contribute and then assume that giving is enough and avoid more compelling and long-lasting action. There is even evidence that such images can lead to forms of arousal and sadism—after all, there are many who enjoy watching others endure pain. How else can we explain the popularity of Saw and other horror movies? Finally, these images can contribute to indifference or even compassion fatigue—that is, a reaction of here we go again, or enough is enough.

Moreover, by portraying victims as innocent and vulnerable, images can contribute to the misplaced belief that these people depend exclusively on the kindness of others because they are too weak to help themselves. But this is far from the case. A post-tsunami evaluation concluded that the vast majority of those who were saved in 2004–5 were rescued by neighbors or local communities, not by international aid agencies.[24] In fact, most local populations have well developed moral economies and decent safety nets that are quite capable of providing effective relief. Sometimes these nets are neither tight nor wide enough to accommodate all who are in need, or they may be overwhelmed by the nature of a calamity. But the assumption resulting from most media coverage is that local capacities never are adequate or that they do not even exist. The resilience of affected populations often defies the image of such so-called helplessness.

For many humanitarians the category of "victim" is politically as well as analytically incorrect because the portrayal of feeble, childlike, immature, and helpless people can have other knock-on, nefarious consequences. It can lead to enhanced dependency (though this problem is possibly more hyped than real). It can interrupt the development of local social contracts and thus help sever the ties between the local population and the state, where real responsibility resides. It can lead aid agencies to justify their power over local populations and to short-circuit the search for exploring local participation.

Although humanitarian agencies have responded to the existence of suffering, their very survival depends on the existence of victims. Philip Gourevitch asks what, unfortunately, is not a rhetorical question: "Does the modern humanitarian-aid industry help create the kind of misery it is supposed to redress?"[25] In other words, a world filled with aid agencies must have a world filled with individuals who are too weak to help themselves so that the "crisis caravan" can roll on.[26] Sometimes this is an accurate representation of the problem, but often times it is not.

Question #9: Do local views matter?

There is a worrying gap between what most humanitarians would say about the crucial importance of input from beneficiaries, on the one hand, and what they tend to do in an emergency, on the other hand. Most aid workers would answer "of course" to question #9. How could it be otherwise? The problem is that the history of humanitarianism suggests that it is usually otherwise. During the nineteenth century humanitarians, like most Westerners descending on colonized peoples, assumed that they knew best. After all, local peoples were not only impoverished, dirty, and illiterate but also were using the same primitive technologies as their great-grandparents. Such backwardness was a sure sign that they were unable to help themselves, and that liberal humanitarians had a God-given duty to help improve the locals' lot. And so, outsiders arrived with new farming techniques that would make locals more efficient, ideas of hygiene that would stop the spread of infectious disease, public health centers stocked with modern medicines that would help cure illnesses, schools in which children would become educated for a more productive life, and technology that would improve daily lives. Humanitarians had much to give, and it was unclear what local populations might contribute to their own betterment—and few seemed to be embarrassed to say as much.

After World War II and with the rise of self-determination, nationalism, equality, and human rights, explicit paternalism gradually became discredited. However, the change in optics and vocabulary has not necessarily meant that local populations were more actively included in various kinds of relief and development programs or even consulted about efforts intended to improve their lives. Especially in emergency settings, aid agencies continued to operate like emergency room physicians, saving lives first and asking questions later. Once the fighting was over and many of the same aid agencies started development projects of various kinds, the attitude among development experts often was that local populations still had relatively little to contribute to planning processes. After all, development specialists were "experts" primarily because they came from a West that already had what these underdeveloped populations hoped to achieve; advanced, specialized degrees and training gave them superior knowledge. Outsiders often spoke of being part of an "international community" with sovereign equality among its member states. All were equal and equally worthy of respect. However, it proved incredibly difficult to translate such rhetoric into practice when some people just might know better.

After the end of the Cold War, the various dominant discourses of superiority were upbraided by numerous factors. First, years of development projects and foreign aid endeavors had not necessarily delivered the goods, and so a widespread critique was that the experts did not know what they were talking about let alone doing. Second, emergency agencies were making some fundamental mistakes that were costing lives, which resulted in adopting and adapting the medical slogan of "do no harm" accompanied by a growing worry that good intentions often led to negative outcomes.

The result from both wide-ranging critiques was the same: development and relief agencies were being told that perhaps they could improve their programs if they more fully incorporated "local knowledge." Furthermore, critiques of the power and lack of accountability in the aid industry led to a growing interest in new forms of collaboration and partnership between international agencies and local populations. A more level playing field resulted for the industrialized countries of the global North and the poorer developing countries of the global South. Local populations were supposed to have a greater voice in determining their futures, an evolution that was heralded as democratic and likely to improve the chances that aid would have a positive impact.

It has proven easier for outside aid agencies to embrace the language of partnership than it has been to operationalize and implement the concept. Some of the reasons can be attributed to the difficulty of teaching old dogs new tricks, especially when the incentives remain for old dogs to keep performing old tricks—money continues to flow from donors to international aid agencies, which remain reluctant to give full partnership on all aspects of the policy process. In short, outsiders are happiest with locals as "implementing" but not as full partners.

In addition to the familiar obstacles to changing unequal relations of power, a normative obstacle also arises: is genuine partnership necessarily good? Those who staff relief and development agencies have received professional and specialized training and are experts not simply because they carry clipboards but also because years of education have given them insights and solutions that are unavailable to those without them. Local knowledge is important in various ways, and locals can be experts in lots of things; but there are times when those with specialized training, especially in scientific fields such as medicine, might know more. For instance, various doctors working for MSF tell stories of how local populations will first go to the local shaman, trained in traditional methods of healing, and only when the patient continues to worsen take him to the MSF clinic. Many staff believe that they could save more lives if somehow local populations would turn to MSF first; and in some instances they start public campaigns, especially when there is an outbreak of, for instance, measles or tuberculosis. But they also worry that they are overstepping their boundaries and pull back—even though by doing so they fear that they are allowing people to die who otherwise might be saved.

The necessity for outsiders sometimes to overlook the preferences of local populations is particularly evident in post-conflict settings. No peace-builder wants to put society back together again exactly as it was—after all, these societies were prone to violence, conflict, and poverty. Instead, peace-builders imagine introducing changes and thereby creating the conditions for peace. But whose vision of a peaceful society carries the day? Should it really be left up to local populations? But what if the loudest and most powerful voices are those of warlords and old elites? Should humanitarians acquiesce when local communities want to keep things as they are, even when they have resulted in mass atrocities? The local villains are quite aware that peace-building will come at their expense, especially when new groups, such as women's social movements, begin to have a greater say. So, should peace-builders team up with local agents of social change even if they are minorities who are not necessarily representative of the majority? In post-conflict environments, peace-builders have the possibility to foster and fast-forward to the kind of social change that almost any objective observer would deem desirable. Is it not also desirable, then, to take advantage of such an opportunity and defeat traditional centers of power that so clearly have worked against the improvement of society?

We roundly criticize paternalism as degrading and ignoring the fundamental humanity of those whose lives we want to make safer, healthier, and better. But are there not times when we want experts to put on blinders, close their ears, and just do what they believe is the right thing?

Question #10: Is humanitarianism universal?

Humanitarianism assumes its universality and claims to operate under the principles of humanity, impartiality, neutrality, and independence. It claims to operate in a world of ethics separate from the dirty world of politics. It claims a cosmopolitan spirit that is not constrained by physical borders.

Yet if we look at the actual history, we cannot help but be impressed by dissents from the mainstream. Although they rarely doubt that their values are universal, aid workers spend a lot of energy attempting to promote what they presume already exists and to persuade skeptics. In other words, the history of humanitarianism is one of trying to transplant values from one place to another, which should stop anyone from jumping on the universal bandwagon. With the benefit of hindsight, it is easy to reject the claims by the missionaries of the nineteenth century who pretended to have a universal appeal; at the time, of course, their arguments were widely accepted in the West. Will future generations offer similar conclusions about the current universal virtues of democracy, the rule of law, human rights, and markets? Asking the question points toward the necessity to analyze all received wisdom, no matter how widely shared or seemingly unassailable.

Although they receive emotional support and confidence from their donors and supporters back home, historically many humanitarians have been received not as gift-bearing visitors but rather as intruders with alien values. "History is never the fairy tale," David Rieff writes, "of innocent victims, oppressive gunmen, and caring outsiders that the humanitarian narrative so often presents."[27] As a recent report regarding the current and future challenges to humanitarianism succinctly puts it:

> Many in the South do not recognize what the international community calls the universality of humanitarian values as such. … Humanitarian action is viewed as the latest in a series of imposition of alien values, practices, and lifestyles. Northern incursions into the South—from the Crusades to colonialism and beyond—have historically been perceived very differently depending on the vantage point.[28]

Although there certainly is not *one* view from the global South, if humanitarianism is increasingly perceived as reflecting globalization and Westernization, there undoubtedly are good reasons why many in the Southern Hemisphere might view aid agencies as the "mendicant orders of Empire."[29] Even those Western aid organizations such as

MSF that do their best to maintain humanitarian space are sometimes treated with considerable suspicion.

What does this mean for the possibility of an international community? Perhaps the best way to relate the complicated entanglement between that moniker and humanitarianism is for each of us to clarify our somewhat opposing views. For Weiss, the so-called international community, though not quite fatuous, is not only an ideology that masks the politics and power that lurk beneath the surface but also an intellectual shorthand that permits obfuscating which actors are actually responsible for exacerbating or mitigating humanitarian problems.[30] If accountability for success or failure is desirable, then it is essential to identify and not hide specific actors whose feet should be held to the fire.

Public international lawyers are at least consistent in relying on the UN Charter for their definition, "peace-loving states." Over time some observers and many social scientists have also included intergovernmental organizations in their definitions of international community because they have been created by the "peace-loving [sic] states." Still other observers have thought it sensible to add to the definition all groups, organizations, and even individuals who are interested in a particular problem; and membership in the purported international community changes over time and by issue-area. A minimal requirement for any community consists of an agreed definition of who is included and a modicum of shared values. Clearly 192 UN member states provide a clear definition by lawyers for membership but fall short on the shared values; and the motley assortment of actors in other definitions means that there is no agreed membership criterion let alone clarity about values.

For Weiss, a 2002 cover of the magazine *Foreign Policy* says it all. A well-dressed man (undoubtedly a diplomat) is standing on the prow of a rowboat and looking through a monocular (or a pirate's telescope) at a totally foggy horizon, accompanied by the caption, "Where Is the International Community?" The main feature continues inside under the overall heading, "What Is the International Community?" The nine essays share almost no common ground, which leads the editors to say in the lead-in: "This feel-good phrase evokes a benevolent, omniscient entity that makes decisions and takes action for the benefit of all countries and peoples. But invoking the international community is a lot easier than defining it."[31] Someday we might have an international community in more than name. But for the time being, it is fantasy not fact.

Although Barnett agrees that those who are most quick to use international community are most responsible for giving it a bad name, he nevertheless argues that the world has seen the emergence of various kinds of practices that reveal the existence of a kind of community.[32] Specifically, if community has any meaning at all, it demands that individuals be willing to come to the assistance of those who are in distress. One of the truly revolutionary developments in world affairs is the expansion of a mutual aid society. If an international community has any meaning whatsoever, it must include a willingness to come to the aid of others who are in distress. As we have seen, there is the hype and there is the reality, and often the reality is not very pretty. But what makes myths work is that people believe them to be true and judge themselves according to them.

What is impressive, in this regard, is not that there is a perfect mutual aid society, but rather that the members of the international community tell themselves that they have a mutual aid society and continue to judge their practices against this ideal. The international community is not perfect. No community is. But enough people believe that there is an international community, and act on that belief, that there is evidence of its existence. In other words, the belief in the international community and the assumption that emergency relief is practically a human right is a symbol of that community helps foster humanitarianism and the international community

After all is said and now written, this book is about the sum of efforts to ensure more frequent respect for the principles of humanity and impartiality. According to an ICRC giant of the past whom we quoted in Chapter 1, Jean Pictet, humanity expresses a general commitment to "prevent and alleviate human suffering wherever it may be found" and to "promote mutual understanding, friendship, co-operation and lasting peace amongst all peoples."[33] Humanity is intimately linked to cosmopolitanism. The claim that each person is of equal moral worth presumes that everyone whose life is at risk deserves equal consideration.

To be a humanitarian, then, requires us to respond rapidly to suffering by others regardless of their identities or locations, to do whatever possible to save lives. Aid workers are routinely celebrated as righteous heroes, as the "last of the just."[34] They are treated as a symbol of what is good about the world and as a model toward which to strive. After a century of ideologies responsible for mass atrocities allegedly to build a more perfect society, humanitarianism's seductive simplicity involves no grand commitment to an abstract ideology but allows a new generation to find solidarity not in ideas of progress but rather in projects of moral urgency and caretaking.[35] To help those crushed by Soviet tanks, to feed the famine-stricken Ibo of Nigeria, to shield the Vietnamese boat people, to save the Rwandans from genocide, and to call for action in Darfur act as moral beacons in a depressingly cynical and nihilistic age.

True, humanitarianism has been, is, and will remain contested. But fortunately there have always been intrepid souls who, unlike their angelic counterparts, have not feared to tread on treacherous terrain in war zones and come to the rescue of strangers. May their numbers multiply.

Notes

Foreword by Jan Egeland

1 Matthew Green, "Eight Foreign Workers Killed in Afghanistan," *Financial Times*, 8 August 2010, available at: www.ft.com/cms/s/0/7452fcec-a208-11df-a056-00144feabdc0,dwp_uuid=be75219e-940a-11da-82ea-0000779e234 0.html

2 Abby Stoddard, Adele Harmer, and Victoria DiDomenico, *Providing Aid in Insecure Environments: Trends in Violence Against Aid Workers and the Operational Response*, Humanitarian Policy Group Policy Brief 34 (London: Overseas Development Institute, April 2009).

3 Jan Egeland, *A Billion Lives: An Eyewitness Report from the Frontlines of Humanity* (New York: Simon & Schuster, 2008).

4 UN Development Programme, *Human Development Report 2009: Overcoming Barriers: Human Mobility and Development* (New York: Palgrave Macmillan, 2009).

5 Human Security Report Project (HSRP), *Human Security Report 2009* (Vancouver: HSRP, 2009).

6 Millennium Project, "Fast Facts: The Faces of Poverty," available at: www.unmillenniumproject.org/resources/fastfacts_e.htm

7 Quoted in Egeland, *A Billion Lives*, 231.

8 "2005 World Summit Outcome," General Assembly resolution A/Res/61/1, 24 October 2005.

9 For further information on the Global Humanitarian Platform, see www.globalhumanitarianplatform.org/ghp.html

Foreword by the series editors

1 Nicholas J. Wheeler, *Saving Strangers: Humanitarian Intervention in International Society* (Oxford: Oxford University Press, 2000).

2 George Orwell, "Politics and the English Language," in *Why I Write* (London: Penguin, 2004), 119.

3 Rory Carroll, "US Chose to Ignore Rwandan Genocide," *Guardian*, 31 March 2004. See also, Samantha Power, *A Problem from Hell: America in the Age of Genocide* (New York: Basic Books, 2002).

4 Michael N. Barnett, "The UN Security Council, Indifference, and Genocide in Rwanda," *Cultural Anthropology* 12, no. 4 (1997): 551–78; and *Eyewitness*

to a Genocide: The United Nations and Rwanda (Ithaca, N.Y.: Cornell University Press, 2002).

5 Among his numerous works, I cite only Thomas G. Weiss, "Governance, Good Governance, and Global Governance," in *The Global Governance Reader*, ed. Rorden Wilkinson (London: Routledge, 2005), 68–88; Thomas G. Weiss and Don Hubert, *The Responsibility to Protect: Research, Bibliography, Background* (Ottawa: International Development Research Centre, 2001), which was a complement to International Commission on Intervention and State Sovereignty, *The Responsibility to Protect* (Ottawa: International Development Research Centre, 2001); Thomas G. Weiss, Tatianna Carayannis, Louis Emmerji, and Richard Jolly, *UN Voices: The Struggle for Development and Social Justice* (Bloomington: Indiana University Press, 2005); Richard Jolly, Louis Emmerij, and Thomas G. Weiss, *UN Ideas That Changed the World* (Bloomington: Indiana University Press, 2010); and Thomas G. Weiss, "What Happened to the Idea of World Government," *International Studies Quarterly* 53, no. 2 (2009): 253–71.

Introduction

1 Philip Gourevitch, "Alms Dealers," *The New Yorker*, 11 October 2010, 105.
2 Ian Smillie and Larry Minear, *The Charity of Nations: Humanitarian Action in a Calculating World* (Bloomfield, Conn.: Kumarian, 2004), 1.
3 See, for example, Mary Kaldor, *New and Old Wars: Organized Violence in a Global Era* (Stanford, Calif.: Stanford University Press, 1999); Mark Duffield, *Global Governance and the New Wars: The Merging of Development and Security* (London: Zed Books, 2001); and Peter J. Hoffman and Thomas G. Weiss, *Sword and Salve: Confronting New Wars and Humanitarian Crises* (Lanham, Md.: Rowman & Littlefield, 2006).
4 US Secretary of State Hillary Rodham Clinton, "World Humanitarian Day," 19 August 2010, available at: www.state.gov/secretary/rm/2010/08/146098.htm

1 Humanitarianism: the essentials

1 Besides Jean Pictet, *The Fundamental Principles of the Red Cross* (Geneva, Switzerland: ICRC, 1979), see David P. Forsythe, *The Humanitarians: The International Committee of the Red Cross* (Cambridge: Cambridge University Press, 2005); Fiona Terry, *Condemned to Repeat? The Paradox of Humanitarian Action* (Ithaca, N.Y.: Cornell University Press, 2002); Thomas G. Weiss, "Principles, Politics, and Humanitarian Action," *Ethics and International Affairs* XIII (1999): 1–22; and Larry Minear, *The Humanitarian Enterprise* (Bloomfield, Conn.: Kumarian Press, 2002).
2 This expression from the late Fred Cuny was first popularized by Roberta Cohen, "The Displaced Fall Through the World's Safety Net," *Christian Science Monitor*, 6 February 1997.
3 Ian Smillie, *The Emperor's Old Clothes: The Self-Created Siege of Humanitarian Action* (Medford, Mass.: Feinstein Institute, forthcoming), quote in p. 15 of draft.
4 Henry Dunant, *A Memory of Solferino* (London: Cassell, 1947).
5 Tony Vaux, *The Selfish Altruist* (Sterling, Va.: Earthscan Publishing, 2001).

6 Stephen Hopgood, *Keepers of the Flame: Understanding Amnesty International* (Ithaca, N.Y.: Cornell University Press, 2006).

7 For the "do no harm" pledge see Mary B. Anderson and Peter J. Woodrow, *Rising from the Ashes: Development Strategies at Times of Disaster* (Boulder, Colo.: Westview, 1989); and Mary B. Anderson, *Do No Harm: How Aid Can Support War—or Peace* (Boulder, Colo.: Lynne Rienner, 1999). For "minimize the impact" see Terry, *Condemned to Repeat?*; and Sarah Kenyon Lischer, *Dangerous Sanctuaries: Refugee Camps, Civil War, and the Dilemmas of Humanitarian Aid* (Ithaca, N.Y.: Cornell University Press, 2005).

8 See James Fearon, "The Rise of Emergency Relief Aid," and Janice Gross Stein, "Humanitarian Organizations: Accountable—Why, to Whom, for What and How?" in *Humanitarianism in Question: Politics, Power, Ethics*, ed. Michael Barnett and Thomas G. Weiss (Ithaca, N.Y.: Cornell University Press, 2008), 49–72 and 124–42.

9 Stephen Hopgood, "Saying 'No' to Wal-Mart? Money and Morality in Professional Humanitarianism," in *Humanitarianism in Question*, 98–123.

10 Hugo Slim, "Humanitarianism with Borders? NGOs, Belligerent Military Forces and Humanitarian Action," Paper for the ICVA Conference on "NGOs in a Changing World: Dilemmas and Challenges" (2003), available at: www.jha.ac/articles/a118.htm

11 For different approaches, see Abby Stoddard, "Trends in US Humanitarian Policy," in *The New Humanitarianisms: A Review of Trends in Global Humanitarian Action*, Humanitarian Policy Group (HPG) Report 11, ed. Joanna Macrae (London: Overseas Development Institute, 2002); Thomas G. Weiss, "Principles, Politics, and Humanitarian Action," *Ethics and International Affairs* 13, no. 1 (1999): 1–22; Ian Smillie and Larry Minear, *The Charity of Nations: Humanitarian Action in a Calculating World* (West Hartford, Conn.: Kumarian, 2004), 192; and Michael Barnett, "Humanitarianism Transformed," *Perspectives on Politics* 3, no. 4 (2005): 723–41.

12 See Nicholas J. Wheeler, *Saving Strangers: Humanitarian Intervention in International Society* (Oxford: Oxford University Press, 2000).

13 We thank Bud Duvall for suggesting this formulation.

14 Hugo Slim, *A Call to Alms: Humanitarian Action and the Art of War* (Geneva, Switzerland: Centre for Humanitarian Dialogue, 2004).

15 See his commentary on "Conservative, or Bourgeois Socialism," *Communist Manifesto*, chapter 3. Cited in M. J. D. Roberts, *Making English Morals: Voluntary Association and Moral Reform in England, 1787–1886* (Cambridge: Cambridge University Press, 2004), 5.

16 See David Brion Davis, *The Problem of Slavery in Western Culture* (Ithaca, N.Y.: Cornell University Press, 1966); and John Ashworth, "The Relationship Between Capitalism and Humanitarianism," *American Historical Review* 92, no. 4 (1987): 813–28.

17 For a review of this literature, see Thomas Haskell, "Capitalism and the Origins of the Humanitarian Sensibility, Part 1," and "Capitalism and the Origins of the Humanitarian Sensibility, Part 2," *American Historical Review* 90, no. 3 (1985): 547–66.

18 Terry, *Condemned to Repeat?*, 245.

19 See Gertrude Himmelfarb, *Poverty and Compassion: The Moral Imagination of the Late Victorians* (New York: Vintage, 1991) and *The Idea of Poverty: England in the Early Industrial Age* (New York: Alfred Knopf, 1984).

20 Hugo Slim, "Global Welfare: A Realistic Expectation for the International Humanitarian System?" *ALNAP Review of Humanitarian Action in 2005: Evaluation Utilisation* (December 2006), 20. Available at: www.odi.org.uk/ALNAP/publications/RHA2005/rha05_Ch1.pdf

21 MacRae et al., *Uncertain Power*, 18–21.

22 See Hopgood, "Saying 'No' to Wal-Mart?"

23 See Stein, "Humanitarian Organizations."

24 Alain Finkielkraut, *In the Name of Humanity: Reflections on the Twentieth Century* (London: Pimlico, 2000), chapter 1.

25 Norman Fiering, "Irresistible Compassion: An Aspect of Eighteenth Century Sympathy and Humanitarianism," *Journal of the History of Ideas* 37, no. 2 (1976): 195–218.

26 M. A. Mohamed Salih, "Islamic NGOs in Africa: The Promise and Peril of Islamic Voluntarism," in *Islamism and Its Enemies in the Horn of Africa*, ed. Alex de Waal (London: Hurst, 2004), 146–81.

27 See, for instance, Ina Friedman, "Jewish Soft Power," *Jerusalem Report*, 24 July 2006, 11–12.

28 Eknath Easwaran, trans., *The Upanishads* (Tomales, Calif.: Nilgiri Press, 1987), 143, 149.

29 See, for example, Michael Battle and Desmond Tutu, *Ubuntu: I in You and You in Me* (New York: Seabury Books, 2009); and Mfuniselwa J. Bhengu, *Ubuntu: The Global Philosophy for Humankind* (Cape Town, South Africa: Lotsha Publications, 2006).

30 See Ephraim Isaac, "Humanitarianism Across Religions and Cultures," in *Humanitarianism Across Borders: Sustaining Civilians in Times of War*, ed. Thomas G. Weiss and Larry Minear (Boulder, Colo.: Lynne Rienner, 1993), 13–22.

31 As with all generalizations, there are exceptions. Some scholars have studied non-Western origins of "just war" theory. For example, see James Turner Johnson, *The Holy War Idea in Western and Islamic Traditions* (University Park, Pa.: Penn State University Press, 1997) and *Just War Tradition and the Restraint of War: A Moral and Historical Inquiry* (Princeton, N.J.: Princeton University Press, 1981).

32 See, for example, John F. Hutchinson, *Champions of Charity: War and the Rise of the Red Cross* (Boulder, Colo.: Westview, 1996).

33 Michael Barnett, "The New United Nations Politics of Peace: From Juridical Sovereignty to Empirical Sovereignty," *Global Governance* 1, no. 1 (1995): 79–97.

34 David Chandler, *From Kosovo to Kabul* (Washington, DC: Pluto Press, 2002), chapter 1.

35 Michael Barnett, *The Empire of Humanity: A History of Humanitarianism* (Ithaca, N.Y.: Cornell University Press, 2011).

36 See David Loquercio, Mark Hammersley, and Ben Emmens, *Understanding and Addressing Staff Turnover in Humanitarian Agencies* (London: Overseas Development Institute, 2006), HPN Number 55, 5; and David Loquercio, "Turnover and Retention: Literature Review for People in Aid," January 2006, 4, available at: www.peopleinaid.org/pool/files/publications/turnover-and-retention-lit-review-summary-jan-2006.pdf.

37 For a good overview of the expansion of the humanitarian sector, see Randolph Kent, "International Humanitarian Crises: Two Decades Before and Two Decades Beyond," *International Affairs* 80, no. 5 (2004): 851–69.

38 These figures are drawn from a 2003 OCHA roster (which no longer is updated).

39 Development Initiatives, *Global Humanitarian Assistance 2003* (London: Overseas Development Institute, 2003), 56.

40 Global Humanitarian Assistance, "03/Global Humanitarian Assistance," in *Global Humanitarian Assistance 2009* (Somerset, U.K.: Development Initiatives, 2009), 14, available at: www.globalhumanitarianassistance.org/analyses-and-reports/gha-reports/gha-reports-2009

41 Rachel McCleary, *Global Compassion: Private Voluntary Organizations and U.S. Foreign Policy since 1939* (Oxford: Oxford University Press, 2009), 16 and especially chapter 1, 3–35.

42 Abby Stoddard, Adele Harmer, and Katherine Haver, *Providing Aid in Insecure Environments: Trends in Policy and Operations* (London: Overseas Development Institute, 2006), HPG Report 23, 16.

43 Peter Walker and Catherine Russ, *Professionalizing the Humanitarian Sector: A Scoping Study*, Report commissioned by Enhancing Learning and Research for Humanitarian Assistance, April 2010, 11–12.

44 For a discussion, see Abdel-Rahman Ghandour, *Jihad Humanitaire* (Paris: Flammarion, 2002).

45 Michael Fullilove, *World Wide Webs: Diasporas and the International System* (Sydney, NSW: Lowy Institute for International Policy, 2009).

46 Adele Harmer and Ellen Martin, *Diversity in Donorship: Field Lessons* (London: Overseas Development Institute, 2010), HPG Report 30, 1.

47 Relief Web, "International: Changes in Aid Pose Challenges," 15 April 2010, available at: www.reliefweb.int/rw/rwb.nsf/db900sid/VDUX-84JSAS?OpenDocument

48 Adele Harmer and Lin Cotterrell, *Diversity in Donorship: The Changing Landscape of Official Humanitarian Aid* (London: Overseas Development Institute, 2005), quotes from 3 and 6, statistics from 7 and 5.

49 Global Humanitarian Assistance, "01/Executive Summary," in *Global Humanitarian Assistance 2009* (Somerset, U.K.: Development Initiatives, 2009), 1, available at: www.globalhumanitarianassistance.org/analyses-and-reports/gha-reports/gha-reports-2009

50 Hugo Slim, "Global Welfare," *ALNAP Review of Humanitarian Action in 2005*, 21.

51 Smillie and Minear, *The Charity of Nations*, 8–10, 195.

52 Global Humanitarian Assistance, "01/Executive Summary," 2.

53 Ibid., 4.

54 Joanna MacRae, Sarah Collinson, Margie Buchanan-Smith, Nicola Reindorp, Anna Schmidt, Tasneem Mowjee, and Adele Harmer, *Uncertain Power: The Changing Role of Official Donors in Humanitarian Action*, HPG Report 12 (London: Overseas Development Institute, 2002), 15. For an overview, see Judith Randel and Tony German, "Trends in Financing of Humanitarian Assistance," in *The New Humanitarianisms: A Review of Trends in Global Humanitarian Action*, ed. Joanna Macrae (London: Overseas Development Institute, 2002), 19–28.

55 Development Initiatives, *Global Humanitarian Assistance 2003*, 1, 14–15.

56 Michael Barnett and Jack Snyder, "The Grand Strategies of Humanitarianism," in *Humanitarianism in Question: Politics, Power, Ethics*, ed. Michael Barnett and Thomas G. Weiss (Ithaca, N.Y.: Cornell University Press, 2008), 143–71.

57 Randel and German, "Trends in the Financing of Humanitarian Assistance," 21.
58 Global Humanitarian Assistance, "03/Global Humanitarian Assistance," 8.
59 Randel and German, "Trends in the Financing of Humanitarian Assistance," 27.
60 Smillie and Minear, *The Charity of Nations*, 145; and Oxfam, *Beyond the Headlines: An Agenda for Action to Protect Civilians in Neglected Countries* (Oxford: Oxfam International, 2003), 2. Also see MacRae et al., *Uncertain Power.*
61 International Federation of Red Cross and Red Crescent Societies, *World Disasters Report 2003: Focus on Ethics in Aid* (Bloomfield, Conn.: Kumarian, 2003), 19–22.
62 Global Humanitarian Assistance, "01/Executive Summary," 4.
63 Smillie, *The Emperor's Old Clothes*, 1.
64 See Chandra Lekha Sriram, John C. King, Julie A. Mertus, Olga Martin-Ortega, and Johanna Herman, eds., *Surviving Field Research: Working in Violent and Difficult Situations* (London: Routledge, 2009).
65 Cate Buchanan and Robert Muggah, *No Relief: Surveying the Effects of Gun Violence on Humanitarian and Development Personnel* (Geneva, Switzerland: Centre for Humanitarian Dialogue, 2005), 7, 9.
66 Carlotta Gall and Amy Waldman, "Under Siege in Afghanistan, Aid Groups Say Their Effort Is Being Criticized Unfairly," *New York Times*, 19 December 2004.
67 Independent Panel on Safety and Security of United Nations Personnel and Premises, "Towards a Culture of Security and Accountability," UN document dated 30 June 2008, available at: www.humansecuritygateway.com/showRecord. php?RecordId=25173.
68 Jan Egeland, *A Billion Lives: An Eyewitness Report from the Frontlines of Humanity* (New York: Simon & Schuster, 2008), 8.
69 Stoddard, Harmer, and Haver, *Providing Aid in Insecure Environments*, 1, 13.
70 Ibid.
71 Laura Hammond, "The Power of Holding Humanitarianism Hostage and the Myth of Protective Principles," in *Humanitarianism in Question: Politics, Power, Ethics*, ed. Michael Barnett and Thomas G. Weiss (Ithaca, N.Y.: Cornell University Press, 2008), 172–95.
72 Nicholas de Torrente, "Humanitarian Action Under Attack: Reflections on the Iraq War"; Paul O'Brien, "Politicized Humanitarianism: A Response to Nicolas de Torrente"; and Kenneth Anderson, "Humanitarian Inviolability in Crisis: The Meaning of Impartiality and Neutrality for U.N. and NGO Agencies Following the 2003–4 Afghanistan and Iraq Conflicts," *Harvard Human Rights Journal* 17 (2004): 1–39.

2 "Birth" and maturation, 1864–1945

1 See Samuel Clyde McCulloch, *British Humanitarianism: Essays Honoring Frank Klingberg* (Kingsport, Tenn.: The Church Historical Society, 1950).
2 Emily Rosenberg, "Missions to the World: Philanthropy Abroad," in *Charity, Philanthropy, and Civility in American History*, 242.
3 Ibid.
4 Amanda Porterfield, "Protestant Missionaries: Pioneers of American Philanthropy," in *Charity, Philanthropy, and Civility in American History*, ed.

Lawrence Friedman and Mark McGarvie (Cambridge: Cambridge University Press, 2003), 49–69.

5 See P. M. Holt, The *Mahdist State in the Sudan* (Oxford: Clarendon Press, 1970), 32–44; and Robin Neillands, *The Dervish Wars: Gordon and Kitchener in the Sudan* (London: John Murray, 1996), 23–34.

6 See François Bugnion, *The International Committee of the Red Cross and the Protection of War Victims* (Geneva, Switzerland: ICRC, 2003), chapter 2.

7 Adam Hochshild, *King Leopold's Ghost: A Story of Greed, Terror, and Heroism in Colonial Africa* (New York: Mariner Books, 1999).

8 Augustus Stapleton, *Intervention and Non-Intervention or the Foreign Policy of Great Britain from 1790 to 1865* (London: John Murray, 1866); Ellery Stowell, *Intervention in International Law* (Washington, DC: J. Bryne, 1921); and Ian Brownlie, *International Law and the Use of Force by States* (Oxford: Clarendon Press, 1963).

9 France's intervention was approved subsequently by the European powers and Turkey. See Stowell, *Intervention in International Law*, 126, 489.

10 The others were: intervention by Austria, France, Italy, Prussia, and Russia in 1866–68 to protect the Christian population in Crete; Russian intervention in the Balkans in 1875–78 in support of insurrectionist Christians; and interference by European powers from 1903–8 in favor of the oppressed Christian Macedonian community. See Danish Institute of International Affairs (DUPI), *Humanitarian Intervention: Legal and Political Aspects* (Copenhagen: DUPI, 1999), 79.

11 Brownlie, *International Law and the Use of Force by States*, 338–39.

12 Stowell, *Intervention in International Law*, 53.

13 Dino Kritsiotis, "Reappraising Policy Objections to Humanitarian Intervention," *Michigan Journal of International Law* 19 (1998): 1005.

14 Ramesh Thakur, "Global Norms and International Humanitarian Law: An Asian Perspective," *International Review of the Red Cross* 83, no. 841 (2001): 31.

15 Brownlie, *International Law and the Use of Force by States*, 340.

16 For a detailed account of Hoover's participation and the bluffing and bravado that he used to establish and then keep running the CRB, see George Nash, *The Life of Herbert Hoover: The Humanitarian, 1914–17* (New York: Norton, 1988).

17 See Emily Rosenberg, *Spreading the American Dream: American Economic and Cultural Expansion, 1890–1945* (New York: Hill and Wang, 1982), 75–77, 117–18.

18 J. Bruce Nichols, *The Uneasy Alliance: Religion, Refugee Work, and U.S. Foreign Policy* (New York: Oxford University Press, 1988), 38.

19 See Louise Holborn, *Refugees: A Problem of Our Time* (Lanham, Md.: Scarecrow Press, 1975); and Kyoichi Sugino, "The 'Non-Political and Humanitarian Clause' in UNHCR's Statute," *Refugee Survey Quarterly* 17, no. 1 (1998): 35.

20 Paul Rabinow, *Human DNA* (Chicago: University of Chicago Press, 1999), 103.

21 Hersch Lauterpacht, "The Grotian Tradition in International Law," *British Year Book of International Law* 23 (1946): 1.

22 For a discussion, see Larry Minear and Thomas G. Weiss, *Humanitarian Action in Times of War* (Boulder, Colo.: Lynne Rienner, 1993), 7–10.

3 The traditional enterprise, 1945–89

1 For discussions of development in world-historical context, see Arturo Escobar, *Encountering Development* (Princeton, N.J.: Princeton University Press, 1994); Frederick Cooper and Randall Packard, eds., *International Development and the Social Sciences* (Berkeley: University of California Press, 1997); and Gilbert Rist, *The History of Development: From Western Origins to Global Faith* (New York: Zed Books, 2002).

2 For an overview, see Richard Jolly, Louis Emmerij, and Thomas G. Weiss, *UN Ideas That Changed the World* (Bloomington: Indiana University Press, 2009).

3 See Gil Loescher, *The UNHCR and World Politics: A Perilous Path* (Oxford: Oxford University Press, 2001); and Gil Loescher, Alexander Betts, and James Milner, *UNHCR: The Politics and Practice of Refugee Protection into the Twenty-First Century* (London: Routledge, 2008).

4 For the story from the person who invented the "package," see Wallace J. Campbell, *The History of CARE: A Personal Account* (New York: Praeger, 1990).

5 Raphael Lemkin, *Axis Rule in Occupied Europe: Laws of Occupation, Analysis of Government, Proposals for Redress* (Washington, DC: Carnegie Endowment for International Peace, 1944), 79–95. For a complete list and access to Lemkin's research, see www.preventgenocide.org/lemkin

6 Michael Ignatieff, "Human Rights as Politics," in *Human Rights as Politics and Idolatry*, ed. Ignatieff (Princeton, N.J.: Princeton University Press, 2001), 5.

7 See Roger Normand and Sarah Zaidi, *Human Rights at the UN: The Political History of Universal Justice* (Bloomington: Indiana University Press, 2007); Bertrand G. Ramcharan, *Contemporary Human Rights Ideas* (London: Routledge, 2008); and Julie Mertus, *The United Nations and Human Rights: A Guide for a New Era*, 2nd ed. (London: Routledge, 2009).

8 This protocol prohibited the use of poisonous gases and methods of biological warfare.

9 For a discussion, see UNHCR, *The State of the World's Refugees* (Oxford: Oxford University Press, 2000), 26–35; Gil Loescher, *Beyond Charity: International Cooperation and the Global Refugee Crisis* (Oxford: Oxford University Press, 1993), 56–71; and Leon Gordenker, *Refugees in International Politics* (London: Croom Helm, 1987), 34–35.

10 For a discussion, see Alex de Waal, *Famine Crimes: Politics and the Disaster Relief Industry in Africa* (Bloomington: Indiana University Press, 1997), 72–77; and David P. Forsythe, *The Humanitarians: The International Committee of the Red Cross* (Cambridge: Cambridge University Press, 2005), 63–68.

11 Philip Gourevitch, "Alms Dealers," *The New Yorker*, 11 October 2010, 105.

12 For discussions, see Alan J. Kuperman, "Mitigating the Moral Hazard of Humanitarian Intervention: Lesson from Economics," *Global Governance* 14, no. 2 (2008): 219–40; and "Wishful Thinking Will Not Stop Genocide," *Genocide Studies and Prevention* 4, no. 2 (2009): 191–200.

13 Gourevitch, "Alms Dealers," 108.

14 See Anne Vallaeys, *Médecins Sans Frontières: la biographie* (Paris: Fayard, 2004).

15 Paul Harvey, *Towards Good Humanitarian Government: The Role of the Affected State in Disaster Response* (London: Overseas Development Institute, 2009), HPG Report 29, 3.

16 Andrew F. Cooper, *Celebrity Diplomacy* (Boulder, Colo.: Paradigm Publishers, 2007).

17 For a discussion, see de Waal, *Famine Crimes*, 106–32; François Jean, *From Ethiopia to Chechnya* (Paris: MSF, 2004), 13–23; and Peter Walker and Daniel Maxwell, *Shaping the Humanitarian World* (London: Routledge, 2009), especially 55–59.

18 Quoted with a discussion in Thomas G. Weiss, David P. Forsythe, Roger A. Coate, and Kelly-Kate Pease, *The United Nations and Changing World Politics*, 6th ed. (Boulder, Colo.: Westview Press, 2010), 47.

19 For a discussion, see Sarah Kenyon Lischer, *Dangerous Sanctuaries: Refugee Camps, Civil War, and the Dilemmas of Humanitarian Aid* (Ithaca, N.Y.: Cornell University Press, 2005), 44–72; François Calas and Pierre Salignon, "Afghanistan: From 'Militant Monks' to Crusaders," in *In the Shadow of "Just Wars": Violence, Politics and Humanitarian Action*, ed. Fabrice Weissman (Ithaca, N.Y.: Cornell University Press, 2004), 66–86; and Fiona Terry, *Condemned to Repeat? The Paradox of Humanitarian Action* (Ithaca, N.Y.: Cornell University Press, 2002), 55–82.

20 See Stephen John Stedman and Fred Tanner, eds., *Refugee Manipulation: War, Politics, and the Abuse of Humanitarian Suffering* (Washington, DC: Brookings Institution, 2003), especially Frédéric Gare, "The Geopolitics of Afghan Refugees in Pakistan," 57–94.

21 See, for example, Larry Minear, T. A. Abuom, E. Chole, K. Manibe, A. Mohammed, J. Sebstad, and T. Weiss, *Humanitarianism under Siege: A Critical Review of Operation Lifeline Sudan* (Trenton, N.J.: Red Sea Press, 1991); and Francis M. Deng and Larry Minear, *The Challenges of Famine Relief: Emergency Operations in the Sudan* (Washington, DC: Brookings Institution, 1992).

22 For a discussion, see Hiram A. Ruiz, "The Sudan: Cradle of Displacement," in *The Foresaken People: Case Studies of the Internally Displaced*, ed. Roberta Cohen and Francis M. Deng (Washington, DC: Brookings Institution Press, 1998), 139–74; and Aristide R. Zolberg, Astri Suhrke, and Sergio Aguayo, *Escape from Violence: Conflict and the Refugee Crisis in the Developing World* (Oxford: Oxford University Press, 1989), 50–55.

23 See Thomas G. Weiss and Larry Minear, eds., *Humanitarianism Across Borders: Sustaining Civilians in Times of War* (Boulder, Colo.: Lynne Rienner, 1993).

24 For a discussion, see Terry, *Condemned to Repeat?*, 83–113; and Jack Child, *The Central American Peace Process, 1983–1991: Sheathing Swords, Building Confidence* (Boulder, Colo.: Lynne Rienner, 1992).

25 This section draws on Peter J. Hoffman and Thomas G. Weiss, *Sword and Salve: Confronting New Wars and Humanitarian Crises* (Lanham, Md.: Rowman & Littlefield, 2006), 25–52.

26 Larry Minear, *The Humanitarian Enterprise: Dilemmas and Discoveries* (Bloomfield, Conn.: Kumarian, 2002).

27 For a discussion of the establishment and evolution of UNHCR, see Michael Barnett and Martha Finnemore, *Rules for the World: International Organizations in Global Politics* (Ithaca, N.Y.: Cornell University Press, 2004), 73–120.

28 See Benjamin N. Schiff, *Refugees unto the Third Generation: UN Aid to Palestinians* (Syracuse, N.Y.: Syracuse University Press, 1995).

29 For a complete discussion of the theories of international relations in relationship to the movement of peoples, see Alexander Betts, *Forced Migration and Global Politics* (Oxford: Wiley-Blackwell, 2009).

30 Michael Maren, *The Road to Hell: The Ravaging Effects of Foreign Aid and International Charity* (New York: Free Press, 1997), 209.

31 Rachel McCleary, *Global Compassion: Private Voluntary Organizations and U.S. Foreign Policy since 1939* (Oxford: Oxford University Press, 2009), 138–39.

32 David Rieff, *A Bed for the Night: Humanitarianism in Crisis* (London: Vintage, 2002), 10.

33 Ian Smillie, *The Emperor's Old Clothes: The Self-Created Siege of Humanitarian Action* (Medford, Mass.: Feinstein Institute, forthcoming), 15 of draft for a conference organized by Tufts University in June 2009.

34 Hugo Slim, *A Call to Alms: Humanitarian Action and the Art of War* (Geneva: Centre for Humanitarian Dialogue, 2004), 4.

35 For a discussion of the changing politics of that time in relationship to Afghanistan, southern Africa, Kampuchea, and Central America, see Thomas G. Weiss and James G. Blight, eds., *The Suffering Grass: Superpowers and Regional Conflict in Southern Africa and the Caribbean* (Boulder, Colo.: Lynne Rienner, 1992).

4 The turbulent post–Cold War era: the "new" humanitarianism?

1 W. Joseph Campbell, "You Furnish the Legend, I'll Furnish the Quote," *American Journalism Review* (December 2001), available at: www.ajr.org/Article.asp?id=2429

2 Nik Gowing, *Media Coverage: Help or Hindrance in Conflict Prevention?* (New York: Carnegie Commission on the Prevention of Deadly Conflict, 1997); Warren Strobel, *Late Breaking Foreign Policy: The News Media's Influence on Peace Operations* (Washington, DC: United States Institute for Peace Press, 1997); and Larry Minear, Colin Scott, and Thomas G. Weiss, *The News Media, Civil War, and Humanitarian Action* (Boulder, Colo.: Lynne Rienner, 1996).

3 John C. Hammock and Joel C. Charny, "Emergency Responses as Morality Play," in *From Massacres to Genocide: The Media, Public Policy, and Humanitarian Crises*, ed. Robert I. Rotberg and Thomas G. Weiss (Washington, DC: Brookings Institution, 1996), 115–35.

4 Milan Kundera, *The Book of Laughter and Forgetting* (New York: Viking, 1979), 7.

5 Philip Curti, *American Philanthropy Abroad* (New Brunswick, N.J.: Transaction Press, 1982), 491–93.

6 William Shawcross, *The Quality of Mercy* (New York: Simon and Schuster, 1984).

7 N. D. White, *Keeping the Peace* (Manchester, U.K.: Manchester University Press, 1993), 34–38; Michael Howard, "The Historical Development of the UN's Role in International Security," in *United Nations: Divided World*, ed. Adam Roberts and Benedict Kingsbury, 2nd ed. (Oxford: Oxford University Press, 1993), 69–70.

8 For a general treatment of the first 65 years, see Thomas G. Weiss, David P. Forsythe, Roger A. Coate, and Kelly-Kate Pease, *The United Nations and Changing World Politics*, 6th ed. (Boulder, Colo.: Westview, 2010), chapters 1–4.

9 Mary Kaldor, *New and Old Wars: Organized Violence in a Global Era* (Stanford, Calif.: Stanford University Press, 1999); Mark Duffield, *Global Governance and the New Wars: The Merging of Development and Security* (London: Zed, 2001); and Robert Kaplan, "The Coming Anarchy," *Atlantic Monthly*, February 1994, 44–76, and *The Coming Anarchy: Shattering the Dreams of the Post-Cold War* (New York: Random House, 2000).

10 Some have argued that there has been an upswing in the number, intensity, and duration of civil wars, particularly since 1989. However, data indicate that the overall quantity of conflicts throughout the 1990s decreased while negotiated settlements increased. See Swedish International Peace Research Institute, *SIPRI Yearbook 1998: Armaments, Disarmament, and International Security* (Oxford: Oxford University Press, 1998), 17. This work is shortened and updated annually by Peter Wallensteen and Margareta Sollenberg in the *Journal of Peace Research*.

11 Norwegian Refugee Council, *Internal Displacement: Global Overview of Trends and Developments in 2009* (Geneva: Internal Displacement Monitoring Centre, 2010), 9.

12 Adam Roberts, "Lives and Statistics: Are 90% of War Victims Civilians?" *Survival* 52, no. 3 (2010): 115–36.

13 For a discussion, see Peter J. Hoffman and Thomas G. Weiss, *Sword and Salve: Confronting New Wars and Humanitarian Crises* (Lanham, Md.: Rowman & Littlefield, 2006), chapter 3.

14 Duffield, *Global Governance; Ethics and International Affairs.*

15 For a discussion, see S. Neil MacFarlane and Yuen Foong Khong, *Human Security and the UN: A Critical History* (Bloomington: Indiana University Press, 2006).

16 UNDP, *Human Development Report 1994: New Dimensions of Human Security* (New York: Oxford University Press, 1994), 22–24.

17 See Rob Jenkins, *Peacebuilding and the Peacebuilding Commission* (London: Routledge, forthcoming).

18 Marina Ottaway, "Rebuilding State Institutions in Collapsed States," *Development and Change* 33, no. 5 (2002): 1001–23.

19 Thomas G. Weiss, "Governance, Good Governance, and Global Governance: Conceptual and Actual Challenges," *Third World Quarterly* 21, no. 5 (2000): 795–814.

20 Roland Paris, *At War's End: Building Peace after Civil Conflict* (Cambridge: Cambridge University Press, 2004).

21 Charles Kelly, "On the Relief-to-development Continuum," *Disasters* 22, no. 2 (1998): 174–75.

22 Duffield, *Global Governance.*

23 David Chandler, *From Kosovo to Kabul* (Washington, DC: Pluto Press, 2002), chapter 1.

24 For a succinct statement regarding the competing logics of relief and rights, see Françoise Bouchet-Saulnier, "Between Humanitarian Law and Principles: The Principles and Practices of 'Rebellious Humanitarianism,'" *MSF International Activity Report* (Paris: MSF, 2002); and Larry Minear, *The Humanitarian Enterprise: Dilemmas and Discoveries* (Bloomfield, Conn.: Kumarian Press, 2002), chapter 3.

25 Chandler, *From Kosovo to Kabul*, 21.

26 Robert Jackson, *Quasi-States* (New York: Cambridge University Press, 1990).

27 Joanne Macrae, "Aiding Peace ... and War: UNHCR Returnee Reintegration, and the Relief-Development Debate," *New Issues in Refugee Research* (Geneva, Switzerland: UNHCR, 1999), 6–7.

28 See Thomas G. Weiss, *Humanitarian Intervention: Ideas in Action* (Cambridge: Polity Press, 2007).

29 Christine Bourloyannis, "The Security Council of the United Nations and the Implementation of International Humanitarian Law," *Denver Journal of International Law and Policy* 20, no. 3 (1993): 43.

30 Th. A. van Baarda, "The Involvement of the Security Council in Maintaining International Law," *Netherlands Quarterly of Human Rights* 12, no. 1 (1994): 140.

31 See, for example, Roberta Cohen and Francis M. Deng, *Masses in Flight: The Global Crisis of Internal Displacement* (Washington, DC: Brookings Institution, 1998); and Roberta Cohen and Francis M. Deng, eds., *The Forsaken People: Case Studies of the Internally Displaced* (Washington, DC: Brookings Institution, 1998). A history of this itinerary is Thomas G. Weiss and David A. Korn, *Internal Displacement: Conceptualization and its Consequences* (London: Routledge, 2006).

32 See Jarat Chopra and Thomas G. Weiss, "Sovereignty Is No Longer Sacrosanct: Codifying Humanitarian Intervention," *Ethics and International Affairs* 6 (1992): 95–117.

33 Kofi A. Annan, *The Question of Intervention: Statements by the Secretary-General* (New York: United Nations, 1999).

34 International Commission on Intervention and State Sovereignty, *The Responsibility to Protect* (Ottawa: International Development Research Centre, 2001); and Thomas G. Weiss and Don Hubert, *The Responsibility to Protect: Research, Bibliography, and Background* (Ottawa: International Development Research Centre, 2001). An updated bibliography and both volumes are available at http://web.gc.cuny.edu/RalphBuncheInstitute/ICISS/index.htm

35 *2005 World Summit Outcome*, adopted by UN General Assembly resolution A/RES/60/1, 24 October 2005, paras. 138–40.

36 For interpretations by commissioners, see Gareth Evans, *The Responsibility to Protect: Ending Mass Atrocity Crimes Once and For All* (Washington, DC: Brookings Institution, 2008); and Ramesh Thakur, *The United Nations, Peace and Security: From Collective Security to the Responsibility to Protect* (Cambridge: Cambridge University Press, 2006). See also Alex J. Bellamy, *Responsibility to Protect: The Global Effort to End Mass Atrocities* (Cambridge: Polity Press, 2009), and Weiss, *Humanitarian Intervention*.

37 Evans, *The Responsibility to Protect*, 28.

38 High-level Panel on Threats, Challenges and Change, *A More Secure World: Our Shared Responsibility* (New York: United Nations, 2004), para. 203.

39 Kofi A. Annan, *In Larger Freedom: Towards Development, Security and Human Rights for All* (New York: United Nations, 2005).

40 Ban Ki-moon, *Implementing the Responsibility to Protect: Report from the Secretary-General*, UN document A/63/677, 12 January 2009.

41 Ban Ki-moon, *Early Warning, Assessment and the Responsibility to Protect, Report of the Secretary-General*, UN document A/64/864, 14 July 2010, para. 14.

42 For a discussion of the politics, see Don Hubert, *Human Security: Global Politics and the Human Costs of War* (London: Routledge, forthcoming). For discussions about the theory of normative advance, see Martha Finnemore and Kathryn Sikkink, "International Norm Dynamics and Political Change," *International Organization* 52, no. 4 (1998): 887–917; Thomas Risse, Stephen Ropp, and Kathryn Sikkink, *The Power of Human Rights: International Norms and Domestic Change* (Cambridge: Cambridge University Press, 1999); and Margaret Keck and Kathryn Sikkink, *Activists beyond Borders: Advocacy Networks in International Politics* (Ithaca, N.Y.: Cornell University Press, 1998).

43 "An Idea Whose Time Has Come—and Gone?" *Economist*, 23 July 2009.

44 "Statement by the President of the General Assembly, Miguel d'Escoto Brockmann, at the Opening of the 97th Session of the General Assembly," 23 July 2009.

45 For an account, see Global Centre for the Responsibility to Protect, "Implementing the Responsibility to Protect—The 2009 General Assembly Debate: An Assessment," *GCR2P Report*, August 2009.

46 Ramesh Thakur and Thomas G. Weiss, "R2P: From Idea to Norm—and Action?" *Global R2P* 1, no. 1 (2009): 22.

47 See, for example, Alan J. Kuperman, "Mitigating the Moral Hazard of Humanitarian Intervention: Lessons from Economics," *Global Governance* 14, no. 2 (2008): 219–40; "The Moral Hazard of Humanitarian Intervention: Lessons from the Balkans," *International Studies Quarterly* 52 (2008): 49–80; and "Darfur: Strategic Victimhood Strikes Again?" *Genocide Studies and Prevention* 4, no. 3 (2009): 281–303.

48 David Rieff, "A False Compatibility: Humanitarian Action and Human Rights," *Humanitarian Stakes Number 1* (MSF Switzerland, September 2008): 41.

5 Turbulent humanitarianism since 1989: rhetoric meets reality

1 Michael Ignatieff, "Intervention and State Failure," in *The New Killing Fields: Massacre and the Politics of Intervention*, ed. Nicolaus Mills and Kira Brunner (New York: Basic Books, 2002), 229–44.

2 Michael Barnett, "The New United Nations Politics of Peace: From Juridical Sovereignty to Empirical Sovereignty," *Global Governance* 1, no. 1 (1995): 79–97.

3 Secretary of State Colin Powell, "Remarks to the National Foreign Policy Conference for Leaders of Nongovernmental Organizations, Washington, DC, 26 October 2001," available at: http://avalon.law.yale.edu/sept11/powel l_brief31.asp

4 Michael Ignatieff, "The Stories We Tell: Television and Humanitarian Aid," in *Hard Choices: Moral Dilemmas in Humanitarian Intervention*, ed. Jonathan Moore (Lanham, Md.: Rowman & Littlefield, 1998), 298, 301.

5 Quoted by Samantha Power, *A Problem from Hell: America and the Age of Genocide* (New York: Basic Books, 2002), 12.

6 Sadako Ogata, *The Turbulent Decade: Confronting the Refugee Crises of the 1990s* (New York: Norton, 2005), 25.

7 Mark Duffield, *Global Governance and the New Wars: The Merging of Development and Security* (London: Zed, 2001), 109–13.

8 Alex de Waal, *Famine Crimes* (Bloomington: Indiana University Press, 1997), 221.

9 Adele Harmer, Lin Cotterrell, and Abby Stoddard, *From Stockholm to Ottowa: A Progress Review of the Good Humanitarian Donorship Initiative* (London: Overseas Development Institute (ODI), 2004), Humanitarian Policy Group (HPG) Research Briefing 18.

10 Andrew Natsios, "NGOs Must Shows Results; Promote U.S. or We Will 'Find New Partners,'" available at: www.interaction.org/forum2003/panels.html#Natsios

11 Quoted in Ian Smillie and Larry Minear, *The Charity of Nations: Humanitarian Action in a Calculating World* (Bloomfield, Conn.: Kumarian, 2004), 143.

12 Feinstein International Famine Center, *Ambiguity and Change: Humanitarian NGOs Prepare for the Future* (Meford, Mass.: Tufts University, 2004); and Antonio Donini, "Humanitarianism in the 00s: Is Universality under Threat?" Paper presented at the 2005 Annual Meeting of the International Studies Association, Honolulu, Hawaii, 1–5 March 2005.

13 Smillie and Minear, *The Charity of Nations*, chapter 9.

14 David Rieff, *A Bed for the Night: Humanitarianism in Crisis* (New York: Simon and Schuster, 2002), chapter 6.

15 Hugo Slim, "By What Authority? The Legitimacy and Accountability of Non-Governmental Organizations," *Journal of Humanitarian Assistance* 10 (2000): 4, available at: www.jha.ac/articles/a082.htm.

16 Andrew Cooley and James Ron, "The NGO Scramble: Organizational Insecurity and the Political Economy of Transnational Action," *International Security* 27, no. 1 (2002): 5–39.

17 Michael Maren, *The Road to Hell: The Ravaging Effects of Foreign Aid and International Charity* (New York: Free Press, 1997), 219.

18 These cases draw on comparisons made in Thomas G. Weiss, "Halting Atrocities in Kenya: Acting Sooner Rather than Later," *Great Decisions 2010* (New York: Foreign Policy Association, 2010).

19 Inga-Britt Ahlenius, "End-of-assignment-report," 14 July 2010, 2–3, available at: www.foreignpolicy.com/files/fp_uploaded_documents/100719_0_ahlenius summary.pdf

20 Sarah Collinson, James Darcy, Nicholas Waddell, and Anna Schmidt, *Realising Protection: The Uncertain Benefits of Civilian, Refugee and IDP Status* (London: ODI, 2009), HPG Report 28, 3.

21 Nicholas D. Kristof, "Genocide in Slow Motion," *New York Review of Books* LIII, no. 2 (9 February 2006): 14. See especially Julie Flint and Alex de Waal, *A Short History of a Long War* (London: Zed Books, 2005); and Gérard Prunier, *Darfur: The Ambiguous Genocide* (Ithaca, N.Y.: Cornell University Press, 2005).

22 UN OCHA, "Sudan: US Congress Unanimously Defines Darfur Violence as 'Genocide,'" 23 July 2004, available at: www.globalsecurity.org/military/library/news/2004/07/mil-040723-irin03.htm

23 "The Crisis in Darfur," Testimony before the Senate Foreign Relations Committee, Washington, DC, 9 September 2004.

24 Roméo Dallaire, "Looking at Darfur, Seeing Rwanda," *The New York Times*, 4 October 2004. See his *Shake Hands with the Devil: The Failure of Humanity in Rwanda* (Toronto: Brent Beardsley, 2004).

25 Julie Flint and Alex de Waal, "Case Closed: A Prosecutor Without Borders," *World Affairs* (Spring 2009): available at: www.worldaffairsjournal.org/2009%20-%20Spring/full-DeWaalFlint.html

26 Center on International Cooperation, *Global Peace Operations 2009* (Boulder, Colo.: Lynne Rienner, 2009), 4, 14.

27 See Alan J. Kuperman, "Darfur: Strategic Victimhood Strikes Again?" *Genocide Studies and Prevention* 4, no. 3 (2009): 281–303.

28 See the entire "Special Issue on the Darfur Crisis," *Genocide Studies and Prevention* 4, no. 3 (2009), ed. Samuel Totten.

29 Gérard Prunier, *Africa's World War: Congo, the Rwandan Genocide, and the Making of a Continental Catastrophe* (Oxford: Oxford University Press, 2009).

30 Jeffery Gettleman, "Symbol of Unhealed Congo: Male Rape Victims," *New York Times*, 4 August 2009.

31 The International Rescue Committee, *Mortality in the Democratic Republic of Congo: An Ongoing Crisis*, www.theirc.org/resources/2007/2006-7_congo mortalitysurvey.pdf

32 Stephanie McCrummen, "Prevalence of Rape in E. Congo Described as Worst In World," *Washington Post Foreign Service*, 9 September 2007, www.washingtonpost.com/wp-dyn/content/article/2007/09/08/AR2007090801194.html

33 Gettleman, "Symbol of Unhealed Congo."

34 Center on International Cooperation, *Global Peace Operations 2009*, 50.

35 Ibid., 52.

36 Ibid., 54.

37 Internal Displacement Monitoring Centre, *The Many Faces of Displacement: IDPs in Zimbabwe* (Geneva, Switzerland: IDMC, 2008), available at: www. internal-displacement.org/8025708F004CE90B/(httpCountries)/B8548DDB 5E6A4450802570A7004B9FD7?OpenDocument

38 World Health Organization, "Mortality Country Factsheet: 2006," available at: www.who.int/whosis/mort/profiles/mort_afro_zwe_zimbabwe.pdf

39 "Zimbabwe Cholera 'Past Its Peak,'" *BBC News*, 24 March 2009, available at: http://news.bbc.co.uk/2/hi/africa/7960674.stm

40 See Swedish International Peace Research Institute, *SIPRI Yearbook 1998: Armaments, Disarmament, and International Security* (Oxford: Oxford University Press, 1998), 17; this work is shortened and updated annually by Peter Wallensteen and Margareta Sollenberg in the *Journal of Peace Research*. See also the reports and updates done by Andrew Mack and members of the Human Security Report Project at Simon Fraser University, first published as *Human Security Report 2005* (Oxford: Oxford University Press, 2005) and *Human Security Report 2006* (Vancouver: Simon Fraser, 2006) followed by annual briefs starting in 2007, *Human Security Brief 2007* (Vancouver: Simon Fraser, 2006).

41 Stephen J. Stedman and Fred Tanner, eds., *Refugee Manipulation: War, Politics, and the Abuse of Human Suffering* (Washington, DC: Brookings Institution, 2003).

42 Kalevi J. Holsti, *Taming the Sovereigns: Institutional Change in International Politics* (Cambridge: Cambridge University Press, 2004), 3, emphasis in original.

43 Rieff, *A Bed for the Night*.

44 B. S. Chimni, "The Meaning of Words and the Role of UNHCR in Voluntary Repatriation," *International Journal of Refugee Law* 5, no. 3

(1993): 442–60 at 444; and Gervase Coles, *Solutions to the Problems of Refugees and Protection of Refugees: A Background Study* (Geneva, Switzerland: UNHCR, 1989), 203.

6 Humanitarianism's past and possible futures: ten guiding questions

1 See Abby Stoddard, *Humanitarian Alert: NGO Information and Its Impact on US Foreign Policy* (Bloomfield, Conn.: Kumarian, 2006).
2 Shannon D. Beebe and Mary Kaldor, *The Ultimate Weapon Is No Weapon: Human Security and the New Rules of War and Peace* (New York: Public Affairs, 2010), 2.
3 Michael R. Gordon, "The 2000 Campaign: The Military; Bush Would Stop U.S. Peacekeeping in Balkan Fights," *New York Times*, 21 October 2000, available at: www.nytimes.com/2000/10/21/us/the-2000-campaign-the-military-bush-would-stop-us-peacekeeping-in-balkan-fights.html?pagewanted=1
4 See Michael E. O'Hanlon, *Expanding Global Military Capacity for Humanitarian Intervention* (Washington, DC: Brookings Institution, 2003); and Conor Foley, *The Thin Blue Line: How Humanitarianism Went to War* (London: Verso, 2008).
5 Adam Roberts, "The Role of Humanitarian Issues in International Politics in the 1990s," *International Review of the Red Cross*, no. 833 (1999): 31–32. See also Peter J. Hoffman and Thomas G. Weiss, *Sword and Salve: Confronting New Wars and Humanitarian Crises* (Lanham, Md.: Rowman & Littlefield, 2006), chapter 4.
6 International Commission on Intervention and State Sovereignty, *The Responsibility to Protect* (Ottawa: IDRC, 2001), xii.
7 Thomas G. Weiss, *Military–Civilian Interactions: Humanitarian Crises and the Responsibility to Protect,* 2nd ed. (Lanham, Md.: Rowman & Littlefield, 2005).
8 Michael Ignatieff, *Human Rights as Politics and Idolatry* (Princeton, N.J.: Princeton University Press, 2001).
9 David Rieff, *A Bed for the Night: Humanitarianism in Crisis* (London: Vintage, 2002), 10, 15.
10 George Orwell, *1984* (London: Penguin, 1983), 230.
11 For a discussion, see Aidan Hehir, ed., "Kosovo: Intervention and Statebuilding Ten Years On," special issue of *Journal of Intervention and Statebuilding* 3, no. 2 (2009).
12 For an overview of the differences between and overlaps among deontological, consequentialist, and virtue ethics, see Marcia Baron, Philip Pettit, and Michael Slore, *Three Methods of Ethics* (Malden, Mass.: Blackwell, 1997).
13 Mary B. Anderson, *Do No Harm: How Aid Can Support Peace—or War* (Boulder, Colo.: Lynne Rienner, 2002), and "You Save My Life Today, but for What Tomorrow? Some Moral Dilemmas of Humanitarian Aid," in *Hard Choices: Moral Dilemmas in Humanitarian Intervention*, ed. Jonathan Moore (Lanham, Md.: Rowman & Littlefield, 1998), 137–56.
14 See, for example, Hugo Slim, "Doing the Right Thing: Relief Agencies, Moral Dilemmas, and Moral Responsibility in Political Emergencies and War," *Disasters* 21, no. 3 (1997): 244–57; Duffield, *Global Governance and the New Wars*, 90–95; and Des Gasper, "'Drawing a Line'—Ethical and Political Strategies in Complex Emergency Assistance," *European Journal of Development Research* 11, no. 2 (1999): 87–114.

15 Marc Lindenberg and Coralie Bryant, *Going Global: Transforming Relief and Development NGOs* (Bloomfield, Conn.: Kumarian, 2001), 76.

16 International Federation of Red Cross and Red Crescent Societies, *World Disasters Report 2003*, 12. Geneva, Switzerland.

17 Tracy Kidder, *Mountains Beyond Mountains: The Quest of Dr. Paul Farmer, A Man Who Cured the World* (New York: Random House, 2004), 286–89.

18 For a discussion, see Peter Walker, "Cracking the Code: The Genesis, Use and Future of the Code of Conduct," *Disasters* 29, no. 4 (2005): 323–26.

19 For an overview, see Peter Walker and Catherine Ross, *Professionalizing the Humanitarian Sector: A Scoping Study*, Report Commissioned by Enhancing Learning and Research for Humanitarian Assistance (Medford, Mass.: Feinstein International Center, 2010).

20 Jonathan Potter and Brian Hobbs, "Foreword," ibid., ii.

21 Walker and Ross, *Professionalizing the Humanitarian Sector*, 2.

22 Stephen Hopgood, *Keepers of the Flame: Understanding Amnesty International* (Ithaca, N.Y.: Cornell University Press, 2006), 13.

23 Stephen Hopgood in oral comments to the authors at the annual meeting of the International Studies Association, New Orleans, 20 March 2010.

24 John Telford, John Cosgrave, and Rachel Houghton, *Joint Evaluation of the International Response to the Indian Ocean Tsunami: Synthesis Report* (London: Tsunami Evaluation Coalition, 2006), 42, available at: www.alnap.org/pool/files/synthrep(1).pdf

25 Philip Gourevitch, "Alms Dealers," *The New Yorker*, 10 October 2010, 105.

26 Linda Polman, *The Crisis Caravan: What's Wrong with Humanitarian Aid* (New York: Metropolitan, 2010)

27 Rieff, *A Bed for the Night*, 54.

28 Feinstein International Center, *Ambiguity and Change: Humanitarian NGOs Prepare for the Future* (Medford, Mass.: Tufts University, August 2004), 55. Also see Feinstein International Center, *Humanitarian Agenda 2015: Principles, Power, and Perceptions* (Medford, Mass.: Tufts University, September 2006).

29 Michael Hardt and Antonio Negri, *Empire* (Cambridge, Mass.: Harvard University Press, 2001), cited in Antonio Donini, "Humanitarianism in the 00s: Is Universality Under Threat?" Paper presented at the 2005 Annual Meeting of the International Studies Association, Honolulu, Hawaii, 1–5 March 2005, 2.

30 For an example of the importance of specifics, see Deborah D. Avant, Martha Finnemore, and Susan K. Sell, *Who Governs the Globe?* (Cambridge: Cambridge University Press, 2010).

31 "What Is the International Community?" *Foreign Policy* (September/October 2002): 28–47.

32 Michael N. Barnett, *The International Humanitarian Order* (London: Routledge, 2010).

33 Jean Pictet, *The Fundamental Principles of the Red Cross* (Geneva, Switzerland: Henry Dunant Institute, 1979). For a discussion, see David Forsythe, *The Humanitarians: The International Committee of the Red Cross* (Cambridge: Cambridge University Press, 2005).

34 Rieff, *A Bed for the Night*, 333.

35 Alain Finkielkraut, *In the Name of Humanity: Reflections on the Twentieth Century* (London: Pimlico, 2000), 91.

Select bibliography

In terms of the traditional principles of humanitarian action espoused by the ICRC and the main UN players (UNHCR, WFP, and UNICEF), good secondary sources are in books in this Global Institutions Series by: David P. Forsythe and Barbara Ann Rieffer-Flanagan, *The International Committee of the Red Cross* (London: Routledge, 2007); Gil Loescher, Alexander Betts, and James Milner, *The United Nations High Commissioner for Refugees (UNHCR)* (London: Routledge, 2008); John Shaw, *Global Food and Agricultural Institutions* (London: Routledge, 2009); and Richard Jolly, *UNICEF* (London: Routledge, forthcoming). And for an overview with particular attention to NGOs, see Peter Walker and Daniel Maxwell, *Shaping the Humanitarian World* (London: Routledge, 2009).

In terms of the nature of contemporary challenges to aid agencies, see: David Rieff, *A Bed for the Night: Humanitarianism in Crisis* (New York: Simon and Schuster, 2002); Mark Duffield, *Global Governance and the New Wars: The Merging of Development and Security* (London: Zed Books, 2001); Alex de Waal, *Famine Crimes: Politics and the Disaster Relief Industry in Africa* (Bloomington: Indiana University Press, 1997); Stephen John Stedman and Fred Tanner, eds., *Refugee Manipulation: War, Politics, and the Abuse of Human Suffering* (Washington, DC: Brookings Institution, 2003); Sarah Kenyon Lischer, *Dangerous Sanctuaries: Refugee Camps, Civil War, and the Dilemmas of Humanitarian Aid* (Ithaca, N.Y.: Cornell University Press, 2005); and Fiona Terry, *Condemned to Repeat?* (Ithaca, N.Y.: Cornell University Press, 2001).

For a discussion of the nature of contemporary wars challenging humanitarians, see: David Keen, *Complex Emergencies* (Cambridge: Polity Press, 2008); Peter J. Hoffman and Thomas G. Weiss, *Sword and Salve: Confronting New Wars and Humanitarian Crises* (Lanham, Md.: Rowman and Littlefield, 2006); Mary Kaldor, *New and Old Wars: Organized Violence in a Global Era* (Stanford, Calif.: Stanford University

Press, 1999); and Robert Kaplan, *The Coming Anarchy: Shattering the Dreams of the Post-Cold War* (New York: Random House, 2000).

For the discussion of donor calculations about coming to the rescue in the contemporary international system, see: Larry Minear and Ian Smillie, *The Charity of Nations: Humanitarian Action in a Calculating World* (Bloomfield, Conn.: Kumarian, 2004); and Rachel M. McCleary, *Global Compassion: Private Voluntary Organizations and U.S. Foreign Policy since 1939* (Oxford: Oxford University Press, 2009).

For a philosophical framing of the challenges, see: David Kennedy, *The Dark Sides of Virtue: Reassessing International Humanitarianism* (Princeton, N.J.: Princeton University Press, 2004); and Michael Barnett, *The Empire of Humanity: A History of Humanitarianism* (Ithaca, N.Y.: Cornell University Press, 2011). Various moral issues throughout the last two decades are found in the journal, *Ethics and International Affairs.*

For discussion of the problems of using military force and the responsibility to protect, see: Gareth Evans, *The Responsibility to Protect: Ending Mass Atrocity Crimes Once and For All* (Washington, DC: Brookings Institution, 2008); Ramesh Thakur, *The United Nations, Peace and Security: From Collective Security to the Responsibility to Protect* (Cambridge: Cambridge University Press, 2006); Alex J. Bellamy, *Responsibility to Protect: The Global Effort to End Mass Atrocities* (Cambridge: Polity Press, 2009); and Thomas G. Weiss, *Humanitarian Intervention: Ideas in Action* (Cambridge: Polity Press, 2007).

For discussions of international relations theory and humanitarian action, see: Alexander Betts, *Forced Migration and Global Politics* (Oxford: Wiley-Blackwell, 2009); Jennifer Welsh, ed., *Humanitarian Intervention and International Relations* (Oxford: Oxford University Press, 2004); and Nicholas J. Wheeler, *Saving Strangers: Humanitarian Intervention in International Society* (Oxford: Oxford University Press, 2000). And for essays about the implications for contemporary social science and research, see Michael Barnett and Thomas G. Weiss, eds., *Humanitarianism in Question: Politics, Power, Ethics* (Ithaca, N.Y.: Cornell University Press, 2008).

Index

CPSIA information can be obtained
at www.ICGtesting.com
Printed in the USA
FFOW01n1650030217
32047FF